To Nancy,

VISIONARY
WOMEN

INSPIRING THE WORLD

12 Paths to Personal Power

Go forth and inspire!

Randy Peyser

Skyward Publishing
Houston, TX

© 2005 by Skyward Publishing, Houston, Texas
info@skywardpublishing.com

Visionary Women Inspiring the World
First printing
Library of Congress Cataloging-in-Publication Data

Visionary women inspiring the world : 12 paths to personal power, project director Kelly O'Neil.
    p. cm.
 ISBN 1-881554-43-0
 1. Women in the professions--United States--Biography. 2. Businesswomen--United States--Biography. 3. Success--Case studies. 4.
Self-realization--Case studies. I. O'Neil, Kelly, 1973-

HD6054.2.U6V57 2005
650.1'082--dc22
2004029867

Cover Design: Heather Mobley, www.truemarketinggroup.com
Editing: Randy Peyser, www.randypeyser.com
Book Design: Doni Underwood, www.coverdiva.com
Project Director: Kelly O'Neil, www.journeyavenue.com

TABLE OF CONTENTS

INTRODUCTION

As a young girl, I had visions of being "big" in the world. I wanted to travel to Europe and explore cultures. I wanted to write poetry and fall in love barefooted while watching the sunset. I really wanted to believe that dreams come true, and that as an adult, I could create a life that I loved. I called it, "my dream come true life."

However, as I grew up, I encountered my fair share of doubts. If this notion was really true, then why weren't more people living a life of their choosing? It wasn't until I sat in a seminar room full of people who had made it their mission to dream big, that I knew, without a doubt, that dreams can come true. My friends make it happen. My colleagues and mentors make it happen. I make it happen.

When I observed that room full of people who were creating this life, I realized that the two main ingredients that were missing for the majority of people who weren't living their dreams generally involved the ability to take action and to feel a high level of confidence related to one's success.

As I grew from a young girl into a woman my visions shifted. I wanted to live on the water, adventurously exploring the world and the people in it, and create a company that supported my lifestyle and honored my values and life purpose. I have since embarked on a mission to create an international conversation about and bringing consciousness of lifestyle to the workforce. I spend my days helping people figure out what they really want to do and how to make money doing it.

I live my life by challenging conventional thinking regularly. I operate at a risk level that is way beyond the comfort zone of many. I used to be pegged by skeptics as someone who didn't live in reality, someone who was frivolous and outrageous. Many thought I wouldn't be successful. Many believed that I couldn't start a business - and when I did – that I would definitely run it into the ground and lose my house. Holding true to the life I chose to create, among the other qualities that were dismissed as "less than desirable," are the very qualities that have made me the success I am today. My company has been named one of the top 500 most innovative companies in America. I have also received numerous, national awards for my work. I now know – for sure – that I can create whatever life I dream of. And I am not alone.

My path to success has taken me on an amazing journey, in which I've had the opportunity to meet and surround myself with some amazing women; women who hold true to their dreams; women who know what they want and who are going to get it. They are not only committed to their dreams, but they are also committed to helping other women commit to and reach their dreams as well. I am inspired by each of them for different reasons. It's these women, among many others, who are collected in this book today to share their gifts of personal power with you. They will provide you with their stories and a way to open the lines of communication to them.

Along with myself, each of these women has a different mission in life. However, the one constant is that we have all learned to harness our personal power to create a 'dream come true life,' and through this book we will share our paths with you.

I am so proud to bring these women's stories to you and to have been touched and engaged by these women myself. I hope that in the following chapters, you, too, will be touched and engaged by them. I encourage you to reach out to them and tell them how their stories have touched you, and how you will do something with the knowledge you have gained to create positive movement in your life or affect the world on a greater level.

Women often shy away from their power. I know because I shied away from mine. I was taught by society that power was aggressive, negative and definitely not ladylike. It's not true. Standing in your own power is a beautiful thing. Being grounded in what you know to be true is power. There's an old cliché, "knowledge is power." I don't agree. Knowledge and action create power.

Not only do the visionaries in this book have knowledge and wisdom – many of them beyond their years – but they've done something with it. They've done something to give back to the world to make the world a better place, to leave a legacy, to inspire other women like you to stand gracefully in your power.

My greatest wish for you is that you embrace every one of these women, as they are all a part of you. When you're touched by a story, you're touched by that story because it resembles a piece of you. When Jenny talks about play, she touches the child in each of us. When Michelle talks about leaving a legacy, she's talking about each of us. I encourage you to see which women you find powerful, which parts touch you, and know that this is a reflection of the power that you hold already inside of you.

It is together that we bring our power to the world. When we openly share our passions, we can then support each other in creating that 'dream come true life.'

To your success,

Kelly O'Neil
"In every community, there is work to be done. In every nation, there are wounds to heal. In every heart, there is the power to do it." — Marianne Williamson

Kelly K. O'Neil
Chief Strategy Officer, UpLevel Strategies
Master Business Coach, Speaker & Author

Kelly O'Neil is the creator of the "Visionary Women Inspiring the World – 12 Paths to Personal Power" project. Kelly is also an avid entrepreneur with a passion for small business success. Kelly believes that people should be doing what they love and getting paid well for it. She has developed programs, classes and products that help entrepreneurs increase their profitability while providing them with the freedom to live their life as they choose.

Kelly is the founder and President of The KateAnn Companies LLC which include: UpLevel Strategies™, Inspiration Place Publishing™, UpLevel Strategies™ and Visionary Women™. Kelly's personal mission is to create an international conversation about building values-based businesses and bringing consciousness of lifestyle to the workforce.

UpLevel Strategies works with small businesses and entrepreneurs to troubleshoot what is holding their company back from ultimate success. Once identified, we teach them a system to take their business to the next level. Businesses at all different stages turn to UpLevel Strategies to participate in Kelly's courses and small group programs to achieve a mastery level of success. Kelly regularly speaks and writes about issues central to small business success. She is currently working on her next book titled "The Conscious Entrepreneur: Strategies to Turn Your Passions into Profits." She was also chosen as a lead coach on the Thrive Media Television production DreamSeekers. It is through her books, public speaking and mentorship program that Kelly is helping entrepreneurs all over the world create highly profitable businesses.

EDUCATION

Kelly holds a BS in Advertising/Mass Communications with a Minor in Creative Writing. She has a certificate in Brand Management Strategy from the Association of National advertisers. Kelly is a graduate of The Coaches Training Institute and is a Certified Dream Coach.

PROFESSIONAL DISTINCTIONS

In 2004, Kelly's company was named a Purple Cow Innovator by marketing guru Seth Godin, citing it as one of the most innovative companies in America. She also received an Addy Award by the American Advertising Association for Brand Identity. In 2003, Kelly received the Compass Award from the Public Relations Society of America recognizing excellence in public relations strategy and execution.

Contact Kelly:
www.uplevelstrategies.com
408.615.8150

Creating a Foundation to Build Your World Upon

By Kelly O'Neil

"If you have built castles in the air, your work need not be lost; that is where they should be. Now put the foundations under them." – Henry David Thoreau

It didn't take me long to figure out that you can do what you are passionate about and get paid well for it. Described as a fierce risk-taker, I am not afraid to dive in and skin up my knees a bit. My attitude is in my work is play big or go home. I love a quote I heard recently that Donald Trump says, "You have to think, so you might as well think big!" That is how I got to where I am today, living the life of my choosing, doing what I love and being paid well for it.

In reading this chapter, many of you might think, "What does this have to do with business success?" My answer is... absolutely everything. I can give you amazing, proven business and marketing strategies that are guaranteed to create a highly profitable business. I can connect you with people in my million dollar rolodex. I can position you successfully as an expert in your field and help you establish your credibility. However, if you don't build a personal and professional foundation under these strategies, eventually your dream will crumble. That is why I chose to focus this chapter. This strategy is "Manage Your Life First, Then Your Business." I guarantee you, you will be happy you did.

The Story of My Journey

I have always been driven. In college, while everyone was partying and taking wild road trips, I started a career in public relations at a boutique agency in the Silicon Valley. Over the years, I developed a very lucrative and thriving PR career, catapulting up the ranks. However, in 2001, after nearly 8 years in

13

Corporate America, I decided I had had enough. As an executive-level communications manager, I had the opportunity to work in many different types of corporate settings, from large Fortune 500 companies, to start-ups, to small business agency environments. This was during the middle of the Silicon Valley Internet Boom, and one day, I hung up my electronic badge and handed in my blackberry, two cell phones and laptop in search of something more.

With a passion for public relations and marketing, I decided to open a small boutique agency that specialized in positioning and crisis communications. Almost immediately, I landed a highly publicized and controversial internet entertainment company.

This company became a very profitable client for me, and Iabsolutely loved working with them. They possessed all of my favorite characteristics for a client: dynamic, fast-paced, challenging, consumer-facing, and they stood for something bigger than their technology; they were going to fight to show America a different perspective by changing the way consumers accessed entertainment.

What is more relevant to this story is the flexibility this client provided me. Due to the handsome retainer I was making with this company, I was forced to make choices about the other business that was coming my way. It was in this time that I discovered the guidelines for the types of clients I want to always work with. Right then, I knew that I wanted clients who would keep me excited about getting up every day to do the work that I am so passionate about. This excitement kept me reeling well into the night and the weekends.

I thought back to other companies and clients that I had worked for – organizations that made me want to pull the covers over my head and question why I had ever gotten into this field in the first place; companies that left me sitting on the couch every night and every weekend in a TV-induced coma, while I hoped that the phone wouldn't ring so I would actually have to move. I mean, really.... what was the difference?! It was all about getting ink. PR is PR is PR, right?

Wrong.

What I learned that first year of self-employment not only changed my career, but changed my path in life. What I realized is that in the past I had completely neglected my values system. I tolerated negativity, lack of integrity, and completely ignored work-life balance. I once again became a slave to corporate America, giving up my life for them. Most importantly, I realized I gave up a piece of my passion and vision every day I walked through the door. I gave up a piece of myself to each client that worked against my value system. The work, that I could love so much, could actually hurt me.

And I wasn't the only one! I had heard horror stories from other consultants and professionals about the culture of businesses and interactions with clients who were lying to the public, giving professionals the run around about payments, or changing a project so much that it cost the consultant money to work for the client. I was surrounded by people who regularly got "the Sunday blues" – the syndrome that occurs on Sunday when you realize you have to get up the following day and go back *there*.

Unacceptable. I realized this nation was in crisis and I was called to do something about it. Margaret Mead's famous quote became my mantra...

"Never doubt that a small group of thoughtful, committed people can change the world. Indeed, it is the only thing that ever has."

Every time someone told me I was delusional to think I could make a dent in a huge problem like this, I recited the quote.

It was in this "Aha!" moment when I realized that I had neglected my values that my purpose in life became clear. My purpose is to create conversations about living and working consciously. Since I have a passion for business and innovation,

15

I made it my mission to support entrepreneurs – especially women – to create success in their lives. I now help entrepreneurs create profitable businesses that give them the freedom to live the life they dream of. I support them in realizing their vision of what they want to create in this world. I found my power and I found a way to manifest it for the greater good of the human race. That was a powerful moment for me.

According to the U.S. Small Business Administration, over 50% of small businesses fail in the first year and 95% fail within the first five years. Included among the top reasons for small business failure are lack of planning, lack of differentiation from competition, and poor marketing strategy.

These figures aren't meant to scare you, but to prepare you for the path ahead. Underestimating the difficulty of starting or growing a business is one of the biggest obstacles entrepreneurs face. However, success can be yours if you are patient, willing to work hard, and take all the necessary steps.

What I have learned from surrounding myself with the best coaches and mentors in industry and having taken the best trainings in the world is that the key to my success has always been inside of me. The most important aspect in my success is the sheer passion I have for what I do and my winning mindset. I live it, and I breathe it with gratitude.

To help entrepreneurs achieve their dreams, I created a strategic system called the Inside-Out Approach – that is proven to create highly profitable and sustainable businesses for my customers. I believe there are three key elements to business success:

Mindset Mastery
Business Mastery
Marketing Mastery

If you are underachieving in any of the three key elements, your business will not reach its potential. Most coaching or consulting firms approach one or maybe two of the key elements. At my company, we analyze and address all three key elements to achieve a mastery level of success. It is the most complete system you will find available today with hundreds of strategies to take your business to the next level.

In my upcoming book, *The Conscious Entrepreneur*, I discuss many of these strategies. However, the first strategy is out of the mindset chapter and is what the chapter of this book is based upon. Fundamentally, it is the most important. My intention is to help you build the foundation for what you are yearning to create so I want to support you in Managing Your Life First and Then Your Business.

"If you don't have you, no one has you." – Kelly O'Neil

One of the biggest mistakes I see entrepreneurs make is to dedicate their whole life to their business. They put their business before their life, letting the chips fall where they may. If the business is doing well, they are happy. If the business is failing, they are miserable. It is possible to direct more positive energy toward your business by honoring your values. By managing life first, your business will become an extension of your life and a support for your desired lifestyle, providing you with an avenue to express your passions. In a small business, you are the business. If you don't take care of yourself, you don't have a business.

The benefits of becoming a professional life manager include:

- ✓ Accomplishing more in less time
- ✓ Greater job satisfaction
- ✓ Preventing burnout
- ✓ Experiencing an increase in energy
- ✓ Developing more confidence
- ✓ Having better relationships
- ✓ Having more FUN
- ✓ Making more money

✓ Reduced stress
✓ Increased long-term success

The first place to start in flexing your life management muscle is by identifying your life's purpose.

Are You Living On Purpose?

"Purpose serves as a principle around which to create our 'dream' lives." — Kelly O'Neil

My belief is that everyone is born with a specific purpose in life. That purpose is different to every individual and manifests itself in different ways. Life Purposes are a state of being, not a goal, and can be as simple as "To Create" or "To Build." For a doctor, a life purpose might be "To Heal." My life purpose is to create consciousness with compassion. My mission is what will make that a reality and I will share that with you in the next few pages.

Your life purpose becomes a guiding beacon to creating a life you love. When you are living 'on purpose' your life will flow more easily. It will appear effortless and you will feel 'luckier' because opportunities will present themselves often. You may feel as though you are contributing to the world and your life will be filled with meaning.

Have you ever felt frustrated with life? Like nothing is going your way? You may have been off your purpose. When people stray from their purpose they feel more frustrated and their life feels like an uphill battle. Everything is challenging. Their life will feel meaningless, purposeless. It might look like they're doing the same thing over and over again without deriving any benefit or joy from it. For example, people might be making money, but they're not getting any gratification from the work they are doing.

A respected colleague of mine, Tim Kelley of Transcendent Solutions, is an expert in helping people find their life's purpose.

18

Tim says, "People already are their purpose all the time, and they and everyone around them are being affected by it. They may not be aware of it, but it's already happening. Getting in touch with your purpose is really about getting in touch with what's already so. It's not a going out and looking and trying to find, or trying to create something." So how do you find your purpose inside?

There are a few methods to finding your purpose. The first method would be to purchase a book on finding your purpose. Tim Kelley calls this purpose hunting. One of the more famous books is *The Purpose Driven Life* by Rick Warren. Another is *The Life You Were Born To Live* by Dan Millman.

According to Tim, "What they tend to do is lead someone through some sort of a process of playing connect the dots. They ask the reader to review her life and look at peak experiences and deduce what those experiences tell her about her purpose. It's a very valuable process. I would suggest to people that they do it with a friend rather than by themselves, because it's very hard for us to catch all the nuances on our own."

Another method to finding your purpose is simply to look inside through prayer or meditation. The final way, and in my opinion the most effective, is to work with a coach who can dialogue with your subconscious, rather than your conscious mind, which is shaped by external opinions.

Whatever method you use, finding your life purpose is the key foundation piece to establishing a fulfilling life and business filled with meaning and relevance. It is the inner framework which determines how you will make your choices. Once you have identified your purpose, fill it in the space provided.

My Life Purpose:

_____

_____

_____

Defining Your Personal Values

"You must stop and reassess your values. You must be willing to be yourself, not what people want you to be because you think that is the only way you can get love. You can no longer be dishonest. You are now at a point where, if you truly want to live, you have to be who you are." – Carl and Stephanie Simonton

A value is a belief, a mission, or a philosophy that is really meaningful to you. Whether we are consciously aware of them or not, every individual has a number of personal values. Values can range from the ordinary, such as the belief in hard work, self-reliance, and punctuality, to more psychological values, such as concern for others, trust in others, and harmony of purpose.

Understanding your value system and how to honor it is a clear path to fulfillment. The key point to keep in mind about values is that implementing a personal values system energizes everything and everybody involved. When you commit to honoring your value system, your life will take on a new energy and brightness, which in turn attracts great success, achievement, and personal happiness. These values can then be applied to your business, causing the same effect with the people within your organization, as well as your customers, products and services, and anyone or anything else associated with the firm.

I personally have made a noticeable improvement in my own life by committing to the values I believe in for me, including integrity, family, contribution, compassion and freedom. If you can identify the values you now believe in, identify the ways you can implement those values in your life, and make a full commitment and effort to apply those values in those areas, you are sure to make insurmountable strides. Life will have a way of becoming more peaceful and your days will seem to flow better.

Over the years, I have had a few acquaintances who did not act with integrity. They constantly made promises they didn't keep, said things they didn't mean and would lie their way out of situations. It used to frustrate me to all ends! I felt so disrespected. It was a continual cycle. They would do something that lacked integrity and I would react with hurt and anger.

Eventually, we would work it out, but it would happen again. By staying in these kinds of relationships I was allowing myself to be a victim. Even though it was their 'lie' or 'cheat,' it was a reflection on their integrity; it was also a reflection on my integrity as well. What I realized is that I was disrespecting myself by not removing myself from those situations and honoring my values.

After I parted ways with those people, my life suddenly became more peaceful. I didn't have the constant struggles I'd been experiencing, and a new space in my life opened up in which I could incorporate new friends who shared values that were similar to mine.

If you are not sure of what your top personal values are, there is an exercise on my site (www.uplevelstrategies.com) to identify your top 3-5 personal/business values.

What personal values are essential for you to integrate into your business? In addition, what are the top three qualities or values you want to own or possess to make your vision real? Some examples are "purposeful," "innovative," "unstoppable," "strong," or "committed."

Because your external world is a reflection of your internal world, what you create in your business will only be as strong as whom you and your employees are inside. Identity is about taking ownership of your vision and for what you want your company to become. Without identity come excuses – all those reasons why you can't make your vision real.

When you choose the qualities you want your business to possess, you prohibit outside factors from slowing you down. You choose to expand your market so you can grow your business. You choose to be a market leader so you can attract qualified employees. You choose to think creatively so you can reduce expenses without sacrificing quality. Your business becomes all about making choices.

My Top Three Personal Values:

1. _____

2. _____

3. _____

Your Personal Vision Will Show You The Path

"One day, Alice came to a fork in the road and saw a Cheshire cat in a tree. "Which road do I take?" she asked. "Where do you want to go?" was his response. "I don't know," Alice answered. "Then," said the cat, "it doesn't matter."
— Lewis Carroll

A compelling vision can help you succeed, be more satisfied with your life, and get the most out of your business relationships. Numerous experts on leadership and personal development emphasize how vital it is for you to craft your own personal vision for your life. Warren Bennis, Stephen Covey, Peter Senge, and others point out that a powerful vision can help you succeed far beyond where you'd be without one. Vision can propel you and inspire those around you to reach their own dreams.

I've learned in my own life that if you don't identify your vision, others will plan and direct your life for you. I recommend setting a 3 year vision. What do you want your life to be like in three years? What do you want your business to look like?

Senge defines vision as *"what you want to create of your - self and the world around you."* What does your vision include? Making a vital change in an area, such as health, technology, or the environment? Raising happy, well-adjusted children? Writing a book? Owning your own business? Living on a beach? Being fit and healthy? Visiting every continent? Helping others with their spiritual development? What are you good at? What do you love to do? What aren't you good at now, but you'd like to be? All of these important questions are part of identifying your personal vision.

When I started my company, my vision looked like being able to support myself by doing the work I loved. I wanted my life to be peaceful and serene, filled with caring and inspirational people. It since has evolved tremendously and I would like to share it with you. I believe by sharing it with you, the chances of the 'universe' hearing me are greater.

My Vision – Written in January 2004

It is January 2007. I heat up a cup of cocoa and wander out onto the deck in my robe and socks, while overlooking the crisp and serene lake in its complete stillness. The scent of pine trees and last night's fireplaces are strong and inspirational. The pups are running in the hills and my husband wraps his arms around me and gives me a warm kiss on the neck as he heads off to work.

My business is very successful. I am earning over $500,000 per year and work less than 20 hours per week in consulting and coaching. I lead seminars several times a year on building successful practices and developing a values-based business. I have written two successful books and am often looked to as a resource for business success in the entrepreneurial market. The clients I work with have developed the courage and inspiration to do what they love and are successful at it.

My life is filled with passion for what I am doing and I am living the life I teach. If I were to die tomorrow here is what I know to be true: I have loved and been loved; I have devoted my life to a purpose bigger than myself; I helped people see what is possible — to live their life with purpose and intention, and reaping the rewards as I have; I have tried and I have failed, and I have tried and I have succeeded; I never gave up; I was true to myself and my beliefs; I have no regrets. I made the most out of every day and could always find a reason to giggle and smile and bring joy to those around me. At the end of my life I want to say that I gave everything I had to give, and had a positive impact, and strove to have a profound effect on the lives of many people.

I contributed to humanity. I gave to those who did not give to me and expected nothing in return. I lived a full life.

Think of passion, values, and purpose as three powerful lenses through which to create, clarify, and enliven your vision. In his landmark book, *The Power of Purpose*, Dick Leider says, *"Purpose appears in proportion to the passion of the energies we expend. It is the passion to make a difference that counts most."*

Passion - what you care about most - is the moving force behind your action. Passion generates emotion and emotions are what energize an endeavor. Emotions and passions set us up to move or respond in certain ways or directions.

Schedule an hour or two for yourself in a quiet and relaxing place. Bring a pen and paper and close your eyes and imagine your life. Ask yourself these questions:

Where are you?
What is your financial situation like?
Who is with you?
What does your life stand for?
What is meaningful?
What are you doing?
What do you really enjoy?
How do you feel?
What do your senses tell you – sight, smell, touch?

Then write a story about yourself in *present* tense as I did in my vision. The subconscious part of the brain only understands now - the present tense - so it is important to phrase

24

your affirmation in the present tense. If you try the future tense, e.g. "I will be happy," your goal will remain constantly out of your reach. It may take a bit of adjusting to get used to writing or speaking your dreams in the present tense, but that is just a formality.

The most powerful thoughts are those made in the first person. When you say "I" you are including all of you; you are integrating and employing your entire being to work toward your goals. It is also always better to make your statements be positive ones rather than negative ones. In other words, instead of saying, "I no longer miss workouts," say "Every time I move it improves my health and my stress level, while returning me to my ideal weight of...."

When you know where you are heading, the choices you make will either lead you toward your vision or take you away.

My Three Year Personal Vision:

_____
_____
_____
_____
_____
_____

Your Mission will Help Manifest Your Vision

In his book, *First Things First*, Steven Covey points out that mission statements are often not taken seriously in organizations because they are developed by top executives, and there's no buy-in at the lower levels. But it's a pretty safe assumption that we probably buy-in when we develop our own mission statements. Covey refers to crafting a mission statement as *"connecting with your own unique purpose and the profound satisfaction that comes in fulfilling it."*

A personal mission statement addresses three questions:

1) What is my life about?
2) What do I stand for?
3) What action am I taking to live what my life is about and what I stand for?

A useful mission statement should include two pieces: what you wish to accomplish and contribute, and who you want to be – the character strengths and qualities you wish to develop. My personal mission is as follows: To leave the earth a better place than when I arrived by creating an international conversation surrounding building values-based businesses and bringing consciousness of lifestyle to the workforce. UpLevel Strategy's Mission is to help entrepreneurs get paid well for what they love to do.

If you are struggling with this exercise, Stephen Covey's site offers a tool to help you build your mission statement: *http://www.franklincovey.com/missionbuilder/index.html*

My Personal Mission Statement

_____

_____

_____

You Are What You Think You Are

Because we create our lives from our thoughts, it is important that we think constructively. Unfortunately most of us, without being aware of it, limit our possibilities for fulfillment because we continually bombard ourselves with negative thoughts. We all carry on some sort of internal conversation throughout the day. I like to call it "The Cruddy Committee." Please feel free to insert more powerful adjectives in this phrase.

Usually if we tune in and listen to "The Cruddy Committee" we find that it is full of negative thoughts and self doubts. Most often we are hearing the voices of our parents, or of people in authority telling us that we can't expect to be happy, that we are bound to fail, that life is suffering and that we should face the stark realities. Out of these negative thoughts arise our self-image and our sense of purpose and direction. With so much criticism and so little sense of possibility, it is clear to see why we never dare dream of better things.

The most important step in truly embracing your personal power is to change your attitude towards yourself and your life. Stand back and listen to the voices in your head objectively and realize just how ill-founded they are. Once you detach yourself from the gremlins in your head, you can begin on the path to self-fulfillment. You are what you think.

Living From Choice

"Decide what your priorities are and how much time you'll spend on them.If you don't, someone else will."
– Harvey MacKay

Your purpose, values, passions and mission create the framework for you to live from a place of choice. You determine how your life will be. It is truly powerful. It is blissfully peaceful. So what does it mean to live from choice?

Living from a place of choice means to consciously choose the results you desire, and to take inspired action to make them a reality. Being at choice is about having the power to say "yes" when you mean YES, and "no" when you mean NO. My business coach, Alan Weiss, uses the phrase, "You have to be willing to accept rejection and reject acceptance." You take charge in your life; it doesn't take charge of you. It's about knowing what you can control, and accepting what you can't. The Serenity Prayer says it best...

"God, grant me the Serenity to
Accept the things I cannot change;
Courage to change the things I can;

and Wisdom to know the difference."

Ever feel as though you're getting in your own way and making things more difficult than they actually are? As though you would have figured it out a long time ago if only you weren't so smart? Living from choice is about choosing to surrender to the natural flow of life. It is about embracing your purpose and the journey you are meant to embark on. It is about learning to swim downstream and gracefully accept the serendipity of life. The ironic thing about the idea of living from choice is....we make our lives so hard by giving away our personal power, and life is so much easier and more fulfilling when we choose to embrace our personal power with compassion.

As a young woman I constantly gave away my power. I let people treat me badly. I let them say mean things about me and I took it to heart. I had learned that I wasn't worthy of the best. I wasn't thin enough. I wasn't smart enough. I simply wasn't good enough. I hid my pain by being benevolent and pretending to be perfect. I gave my power to the pain.

In October of 2002, after a tremendously painful breakup with a man who I loved with all of my soul, a friend suggested I do something for myself to get out of the house and take my mind off things. I booked a massage at a spa with a woman I had never met. Her name was Ronnie.

As I lay on her table and Ronnie began to massage me, she commented on how tense I was. I told her I had just gone through a breakup. As she worked her magic on my tense muscles she told me she could feel the anguish inside of me. Tears started to silently role down my face as she asked me about what had happened. Not allowing to let myself be vulnerable (which at the time I associated with being weak), I normally wouldn't have opened up. The strange thing is, her compassion for me as a woman was so sincere that I openly wept on the table, telling her of my broken heart and soul. What she said to me next is permanently engraved on my soul forever.

As I lay face up on the table with tears streaming down my cheeks and into my ears, Ronnie leaned down at the back of

28

the table with her forehead to mine and whispered, "You are a woman with tremendous heart and strength. This time will only make you stronger and teach you to love more compassion- ately. You will use the strength created from all of the pain in your life to make a difference in this world. Women like you are a gift to my daughters and yours. You are a gift to the world. Embrace your gift and use it for its intended purpose."

At the end of her sentence, she placed her hands on my cheeks to dry my tears and kissed me on the forehead. I felt a blazing ball in the center of my body that I now attribute to being my personal power. She exited the room and I got dressed and left in a haze of bewilderment concerning what had just occurred.

A few days later, I went back to tell Ronnie how much our conversation had meant to me, only to discover that she was gone with no forwarding address. I have never been able to find her since.

I believe Ronnie was one of my soul's messengers. She was an angel who blessed me with compassion and grace as she spoke to my soul. I will never forget the impact she had on my life. My intention is to use this gift that I have been given and to share it with each and every one of you. You, too, are a gift.

"We advance on our journey only when we face our goal, when we are confident and believe we are going to win out."
– Orison Swett Marden (1850 - 1924)

May your journey be filled with happiness and success.

Kelly O'Neil
Founder & President, UpLevel Strategies

Christine Kloser
Founder and Executive Director of NEW
Entrepreneurs, Inc
Author of *Inspiration to Realization*

Christine Kloser is the Founder and Executive Director of NEW Entrepreneurs, Inc. (Network for Empowering Women Entrepreneurs), Author of *Inspiration to Realization*, and a coach and speaker who helps women reach for success. Admired for the impact she has made on countless numbers of women, she has been honored by the Westside Women's Network, at WomenSpeak, A Celebration of the Way Women Work.

Christine has coached hundreds of people to take charge of their personal, financial, spiritual and business lives through her 10-week group coaching programs and private sessions. She is recognized as a pioneer who bridges the gap between business and spiritual fulfillment. A sought after speaker, she has also been a guest on numerous national radio and television shows, and her articles and quotes appear in a variety of publications from coast to coast.

In addition, she is a proud member of the Who's Who of Empowering Executives and Professionals, and the founder of Empowered Women Entrepreneurs Day. Christine also hosts her own television program in Los Angeles.

For More Information:

NEW Entrepreneurs, Inc.
P. O. Box 661274
Los Angeles, CA 90066
Ph: 310.745.0794
Fax: 310.745.0841
ck@newentrepreneurs.com
www.NEWentrepreneurs.com

Follow Your Heart: The Only Path to Fulfillment

By Christine Kloser

Have you ever had a nagging feeling that if you don't change your life drastically, you'll end up living someone else's life instead of your own? This was the feeling I had in April 1988 when I was about to graduate from college. Up until that time, I had always done what was expected of me. I was a competitive figure skater, jazz dancer, an average student, and a pretty agreeable, disciplined young woman. I had been happy with the status quo until I began to think about life after college.

Maybe you've asked yourself the same questions I asked of myself at that time. What was I going to do for a living? What would make me happy? How would I know if I was doing what I was meant to be doing? What if nobody wanted to hire me? How would I keep a roof over my head? What would it take to succeed? What would it take for me to feel fulfilled? Where did I belong?

One thing I knew for sure was that I didn't belong in New England. I don't know where it came from, but I felt an urge to get out of town and start a new life – a life that I designed for myself and that wasn't dictated by what society thought I should do. For example, society wanted me to dress up in a business suit and go to on-campus interviews, which I did once. I disliked it so much I vowed never to do that again. And, I didn't.

Thankfully, the excitement and trepidation of college coming to an end made me look deeper to see what was right for me. I knew a lot about what I didn't want, but I had no idea what I did want. I didn't want to live a traditional, conservative life working for some big company that gave me great benefits. Even then, I knew there was something bigger for me. But, what was it? This felt like a major crossroads at the ripe old age of 21. But, it was the beginning of the journey of following my heart.

Have you ever had those moments? The moments where life forces you to take a close look inside of your heart and soul? Yes, those moments are the moments you begin to discover your true answers.

What was my true answer? I can remember the exact scene when my answer came. Believe it or not, I was sitting at the bar in my favorite college pub with one of my friends. I still don't know where the idea came from, but over a pitcher of beer, we decided to move to sunny San Diego after graduation. It felt so right, and to this day, I know my decision to move was the first time I dared to listen to my heart and follow it.

Take a moment right now and reflect on your own life. Can you identify the first time you followed your heart, or at least the first time you felt your true heart's desire calling to you?

Why San Diego? Who knows? My friend and I enrolled another girlfriend to move with us and the plans began. I can honestly say my life would never be what it is today if I hadn't made this leap of faith. I moved without a job, without a place to live, and without knowing a single person who lived in San Diego, except for the two friends who were moving with me. I guess you could call it destiny; I call it following my heart, and it felt great to take this big step to lay down a path to becoming who I am today.

What major decisions have you made in your life to lay down the only path to your fulfillment? Maybe you ended a bad relationship, started a business, discovered your dream job, or quit it all to be a stay-at-home Mom. If you begin to look at the decisions in your life that have lead to your greatest reward, you'll discover those decisions probably came from your heart, rather than your head. Your heart is the best place for a decision to come from.

There's a place inside everyone who knows what is right for them. For me, it was saying "good-bye" to my family and friends in Connecticut, and saying "hello" to California. The greatest joy of following my heart in 1988, was to know that I actually could follow my heart. I learned I was willing to risk big to win big, and to not be afraid of the unknown. Maybe all those years of competitive figure skating and being alone on the ice in front of judges built my confidence and helped me realize that I could risk, and maybe even fail, without thinking I was a failure.

The concept of failing without considering yourself a failure is one of the key elements in becoming confident to follow your heart. If you're constantly afraid of failing or feeling like a failure, you'll never take a chance on your dream. Failure is one of the best ways to succeed because it teaches you what didn't work and brings you one step closer to what will.

Take a look at the most successful people you know. Chances are they followed their heart, took risks, failed several times and simply kept on going. The only failures are people whose dreams get buried with them.

What is the real risk in following your heart? Yes, failure is one risk, but you know now that failure is practically a necessity if you're going to experience success. Looking like a fool is another risk. What will people think if you follow your heart and try something new and it doesn't work? They may look at you with judgment, disapproval or worry. The thing they don't know is that people who follow their heart aren't concerned with what other people think about them.

Contemplate this for a moment. Have you ever not done something because of what others might think of you? Chances are, like me, you've lived to regret those decisions. As long as we're eliminating risks in following our heart, what are some other risks we can dispel? How about this one? "I don't know how." Perhaps you've thought about following your heart and want to start a new business, buy your first investment property, or start a family. Here's something to think about. Did Thomas Edison know how to make a light bulb when he started? No. Did Alexander Graham Bell know how to make a telephone when he started? No. Does anyone know how to do something big before they start? Chances are, they don't. The point? Don't wait until you know what to do to get started in fulfilling your heart's desire because chances are you'll never know enough. Get started on your dreams, and trust that you will learn what you need in order to become successful.

This has been one of the greatest lessons to propel me to success. If I waited until I knew 'enough' you certainly wouldn't be reading my story in the pages of this book. Maybe you're asking what happened after I moved to California. It's a long story with lots of risk, my fair share of failure, and a tremendous amount of success. It all began by listening to my heart and soul to guide me from one endeavor to another.

Before I share the rest of my story, I want to tell you that in my early twenties, I couldn't have dreamed of living the life I'm living right now. It's better than I ever imagined. I'm doing work I love. I have a great marriage, and right now, as I write this chapter, I'm sitting poolside at my favorite spa in Ojai, California. I can honestly say it doesn't get much better than this. For me, for you, for everyone on earth, the key to unlocking the door to your personal paradise and your only path, is inside your heart.

So, how did my heart get me from being a new college graduate driving cross-country in a tiny VW, to becoming the Founder and Executive Director of the Network for Empowering Women Entrepreneurs, author of *Inspiration to Realization*, speaker, coach and seminar producer? For starters, I landed a temporary job in San Diego with a great rock and roll radio station. The job was supposed to be for two months and ended up being an eight month assignment instead. When the assignment ended, my heart told me it was time to go back to Connecticut and get a real job.

I followed my instinct back to the East Coast, and believe it or not, ended up falling into an Account Executive position at the top radio station in Connecticut. I applied for a job as an Administrative Assistant and they hired me as an Account Executive. It was awesome, until the new management came in and I got fired. But, as luck would have it, one of my competitors hired me instantly because I had taken away a lot of their business while I was at the other station. What comes around goes around, and I soon had all of my advertisers as clients for the new station I worked for.

As destiny would have it, I fell in love with a man who was moving to Los Angeles and who wanted me to move there with him. So, once again, there I was in a car driving cross-country to Southern California. Of all things, this time I was going to be a nanny. At least that was how my Los Angeles life began. Of course, following my heart, I stayed in Los Angeles after the guy quickly dumped me.

I have no real idea why I stayed, besides to say that I truly felt like the only path I could take: to stay and be guided to my next perfect endeavor. At this stage of my life, I listened more closely to my heart and knew I needed to find other part-time work while I was a nanny. So, I started teaching aerobics at a local women's gym (which was something I had done since I was 17) and also got a sales job for a local educational center.

Somehow I knew I needed to be prepared to support myself if my nanny job didn't work out. Wow, was I glad my heart told me that one. I ended up being owed thousands of dollars by the family I worked for, and literally packed up and moved out in three hours.

I was fortunate to have made friends at my sales job who invited me to move in with them until I found my own place. As fate would have it, one of those friends knew a personal trainer, who suggested I look into becoming a trainer myself. It sounded good to me and felt right in my heart at the time. With very little effort, I landed a great personal training job at the same gym where I was already teaching aerobics.

My business grew quickly until I had enough of a clientele to quit my sales job and step out on my own. I moved into my own apartment, and opened a home-based personal training business. I was blessed to never have a shortage of wonderful clients.

One thing led to another. I continued to follow my heart and I could feel myself getting closer to finding my true calling. So far, my heart had guided me on a very easy and effortless path. I always had plenty of money, didn't have to work very hard, and had a very active social life. I even ended up becoming a competitive Country-Western dancer and won competitions throughout the United States, including one which was on live national television.

The next part of my path, however, was the most challenging part I could have imagined, but it was also the most valuable piece I needed in the process of becoming who I am today, and truly feeling like I am fulfilling my destiny.

As you read through the next part of my story, I invite you to look at the challenges you've had in your own life, perhaps the ones that felt like you were even betrayed by following your heart. Look further, and as you'll read below, I'm sure you'll discover the challenges were exactly what you needed to bring you into the next phase of your life.

In 1995, my heart brought me to discover yoga as a personal practice. I loved it so much that I began to convert my personal training clients into private yoga clients. They loved it too. I ended up teaching at a very popular studio in Los Angeles, where I met a student who invited me to open my own private yoga studio and personal training gym in an office building he owned. That was 1998. I jumped at the opportunity and opened my first retail business.

I had no idea I would end up working twelve-hour days, sometimes seven days a week. Challenging, indeed. But, it was through this experience that I learned what hard work meant. My friends thought I was nuts for working so hard, and I was beginning to think the same thing because I didn't know anyone else who owned their own business. I didn't know how challenging entrepreneurship could be.

Thankfully, I had developed great leadership skills through a volunteer women's organization I had joined in 1995. I decided to merge my leadership skills with my need to be connected with other like-minded, women business owners. In April 2000, I brought together a group of five friends for dinner in the back of a Chinese restaurant to share my vision of creating a place where women entrepreneurs could meet to be inspired, educated and motivated to stay on their path to success. We kept meeting every month, thank goodness, because the challenges I had up until this point in business were nothing compared to what lay ahead.

The Universe has a perfect way of giving you the experience you need to become everything you're meant to be in this world, and the Universe brought me a dream opportunity that ended up being too good to be true. It was a miracle, I thought. Through a series of connections in my community, I ended up being given a larger yoga studio in a very upscale neighborhood in Los Angeles. All I had to do was take over the lease – to the tune of $3,500+ per month. I didn't think through the numbers logically, because it seemed like a good idea and a challenge I wanted to take on. My heart told me it was a good opportunity. I imagined it would also be a good financial opportunity because I could fit five times the number of students in this space than I could in my original yoga studio. I crunched the numbers loosely and made a quick decision to go for it.

Thankfully, by this time in my life, I had met the man who I would marry. We were engaged to be married soon after I took over this larger studio, and I had no idea how much I would need him in the coming three years. He actually took over the yoga studio operations after our wedding so I could focus full-time on my other growing business. I know I couldn't have done it without him.

I'd like to say that I wish I hadn't decided to take over the larger yoga studio, but the truth is it taught me some very valuable lessons, and I am grateful for every challenge I had. You see, the new yoga business, which I had for three years, cost me more money and peace of mind than I knew possible. Once we realized we couldn't turn the business around, and had drained all of our savings (and then some), we decided to sell the business.

After almost a year of negotiations with a great buyer, and discovering some permitting issues that weren't disclosed when I had taken over the business, we lost the sale and were devastated. By far, this was the most challenging time of my life. We set a date to lock the doors and possibly file for bankruptcy because we couldn't pay the rent. By the grace of God, and always keeping faith that this was all happening for a reason, we were literally saved by a last minute investor who took over the lease payments and rescued us from what had become our 'sinking ship.'

I cannot begin to fully explain how challenging this time was, but if you've every gone through a financial challenge in your life, had to call your vendors to make special payment arrangements, learned how to play 'beat the bank' when paying bills, and prayed every day for a miracle, then you have some sense of the challenge my husband and I faced.

The good news in this story is that I am a stronger and better business woman because of it. I have more compassion for people who are experiencing challenges, and I have a much deeper belief in the good of the Universe, as well as the feeling that I am Divinely guided and protected. My heart did know exactly what I needed to further me on my soul's perfect path, but it came wrapped in a package that looked very different than what I ever could have expected.

When you think back on a challenging time, did you also experience a positive parallel experience in another area of your life? I just spoke with a client yesterday who was talking about this very thing. One part of her life was extremely challenging, while another part of her life was expanding and growing at a very exciting pace.

When you are following your heart and letting it guide you from one experience to another, you may find the challenging times sprinkled with absolute bliss. This is how I knew I was truly listening to my heart. In the middle of the devastation of the yoga studio, I was also experiencing my greatest and most fulfilling success, which was with the Network for Empowering Women Entrepreneurs.

Remember my small group of five friends that met monthly in the back of the Chinese restaurant in April 2000? They were my saving grace through the challenging times of the yoga business. This small group of women, over the course of three years, had organically grown to seventy-five women who met monthly. I had started a full-fledged, professional organization for women entrepreneurs, a seminar company, a worldwide email newsletter and publishing company and had attracted hundreds of members.

Yes, I had become the Founder and Executive Director of this grass roots movement to bridge the gap between women's business lives, personal lives, spiritual lives, and financial lives. The organization was officially named the Network for Empowering Women Entrepreneurs and opened for membership in 2001.

Was this something I had set out to do? Absolutely not. Was it my calling? It sure felt like it. Was I fulfilled in this work? Yes. Did I have a budget for marketing or advertising? No. How did it grow so quickly and easily? I'd have to say it was because I followed my heart.

Maybe you can relate to this experience if you've ever found yourself doing something incredibly fulfilling, rewarding, and profitable, and thought to yourself, 'how did this all happen?' My belief is that when you're truly listening, following your heart, and have a clear vision of what you want to create and how you'll be of service to others, the Universe will come to help you in miraculous ways.

Now, I'm grateful to say that I direct the Network for Empowering Women Entrepreneurs, and run my coaching practice full-time. I am a successful seminar producer, speaker, author and publisher and enjoy a huge network of like-minded women.I'm in the process of letting go of everything that doesn't bring me absolute joy as my husband and I prepare to bring in a family.

40

Sitting where I sit now (poolside at Spa Ojai) I feel an extreme sense of gratitude and joy that I have followed my heart, no matter what. I was willing to do whatever it took to live the life I'm living now. Even when I didn't know where my heart was taking me, even when it led me to some very dark places, I always knew I would find and fulfill my true destiny.

Your heart is like a compass. It knows the way if you allow it to show you. Be mindful, however, not to abandon your heart's desire when you experience challenges. Your heart knows what you need to become the best possible 'you' you can be.

Until I experienced the challenges of my second yoga studio, I had felt blessed because everything came so easily for me. I needed to learn that the easiest way isn't necessarily the best way. The challenges showed me what I was made of. I learned to ask for help, to be willing to share my failure with people, and to find that I was still loved, accepted and valued for who I was. My heart led me to realize that I am more than my accomplishments and my achievements, and you are too.

Your heart knows what is best for you. Allow yourself to trust it. Ask for its input. Ask how it feels about a decision and it will guide you. Whatever you dream of is yours for the asking. That's not to say it will be handed to you on a silver platter. But it will be given to you if you maintain your faith and continue to be guided by your true desire. Somehow, miracles will appear, and you will see signs that you are on your right path.

Ask yourself, what is the Universe trying to tell me through my heart? Am I truly open to following my heart and to learning the lessons I'm meant to learn? Am I open to receive the blessings, too?

I invite you now to look back on the experiences of your life, including the challenging ones, and begin to see the thread of hope and possibility that was always present even in the darkest of times. That was your heart guiding you.

If you find it difficult to remember the major experiences of your life, use a timeline. Draw a graph with one line going vertically at the left of your page. Then draw another line going horizontally at the center of the vertical line. It should look like a sideways capital letter 'T.' At the left horizontal line, write your- birth year; at the right side of the horizontal line, write the current year. At the top of the vertical line write "peak experiences." At the bottom of the vertical line write "challenging experiences." Now, place your pen where the horizontal and vertical lines meet and begin to chart the experiences of your life, the good ones and the bad ones. It will end up looking like an EKG report, or a seismograph report, with peaks and valleys.

The main thing to notice is how the challenging times at the bottom of the graph are most likely followed by a wonderful growth opportunity that leads to peak experiences in the top half of the graph. As long as you keep moving forward, and continue to follow your heart and are open to learning every- thing you're meant to learn through the good times and the challenging times, you will reach your destiny. You will experi- ence a truly fulfilling and heart-centered life. Your heart truly is your compass. Let it point you in the direction of your dreams.

Wendy Robbins
Co-Inventor of 'The Tingler' Head Massager
& Co-Founder of everything for love.com Inc. &
Founder of Nowhere To Millionaire

Wendy Robbins and her business partner (in debt $10,000) made millions in 2 years by developing The Tingler – head massager. Wendy and/or her products have been featured in/on Ellen, Montel Williams, CNN, Live with Regis and Kelly. Wendy has co-authored/contributed to 4 books, one with Donald Trump and Susie Orman, featured in new best selling book, by Mark V. Hansen and Bob Allen.

An international speaker, Wendy is the creator of "Sleep Your Way To Success" (software to reprogram old, limited programs so listener becomes limitless and creates everything desired) and "Why Marry A Millionaire? Just Be One!" – which teaches how to obtain a millionaire mindset and "Show Me The Money Success System" – focusing on bringing products to market.

Learn to make money, to have a fulfilling, passionate life and get a FREE $197 gift. Visit www.nowheretomillionaire.com – Available for speaking and coaching.

P.S – The chapter in this book is from Wendy's upcoming book, "Why Marry A Millionaire? Just Be One!

Wendy Robbins
(866) 293 - 1984
wendy@nowheretomillionaire.com
www.nowheretomillionaire.com
www.everythingforlove.com

The Little You - You Who Could

By Wendy Robbins

I used to be my dad. I embraced anger, struggle, conflict, and fear of intimacy, and I defended a deep rooted belief in separation. I was full of made up rules, should's, have to's, stuck, rigid, and unkind to myself.

I was also my mother. I hid, feared, shut down, and didn't express my feelings. I couldn't identify any of them except numbness.

They were great teachers.

I left home at 14. My heart was hard, armored and afraid. I pretended I was tough. I didn't believe in the word, 'trust,' and did everything I could to stay asleep. I believed all the stories I told about being hurt, sad, and a victim. I got sympathy from those tales. People seemed to love misery – they had equally "sad" stories that held them small, too.

It is easy to hide when mass hypnosis is prevalent and we think it's healthy to be dysfunctional. I made challenges where there weren't any. I created boundaries upon boundaries to protect my tender heart. Finally, I decided it was too hard and boring to hide anymore. So I ventured below the conditioning, beyond my programming and inner robot, and discovered I had the strength to tell the truth and to stop lying to myself.

I learned who I was being in the world was not who I truly am. I began discovering who I am. That conversation holds my attention. I imagine it will hold yours, too.

When I began, I cried for the first time in years; I honestly couldn't identify who my authentic self was. I had so many masks, so many veils, and an outgoing personality. People liked me and that's all that counted. If someone *out there* liked me, I figured that I must be OK *in here*. I was addicted to being liked, being accepted, and being successful – meaning, making a lot of money. Everything else was secondary.

I've discovered it's painful to reveal myself at times; yet it's harder to hide out, not feel, and avoid intimacy. I choose to explore the stuff I run away from. I deal with the hurt, sadness, blame, rejection to awaken compassion. I replace toughness by breaking the heart wide open and softening. I make friends with what I reject in myself and others. I trust that through breakdown there is breakthrough. The truth is that I'm not always wanting to be who I am. Can you relate to any of that?

Think about this: do you know who you are? Truly. Not the pretend version. Not the dainty dance done to get the applause. Not the show put on to be accepted. Anything but being rejected one more time, huh?!

Under the thick deception lives the child. The innocent. The vulnerable. The awkward. The naked. The one who is committed to tell the truth no matter what the 'cost or consequence.' The one who is simply herself, steadfast, in grace, and who has radical acceptance for who she is. She doesn't care at all what others think.

Change isn't hard. It's easy to shift when you have nothing to defend and are open to be free. I promise that if I can do it, you can too!

In the process of answering that primal question, "Who am I?," I let go of any preconceptions and anything that fights for limitations. Anything that tells me I am not truly divine is let go of.

This process involves a lot of risk. It's not comfortable. It takes courage, mindfulness and the desire to know nothing. It goes against everything we are taught. What we are told is natural is no longer natural to me. I believe in having healthy self-esteem. I accept that I love myself – my ego and divinity are holding hands and integrating into a compelling life dream story.

They don't teach what I am speaking about in most schools, families, or churches or synagogues. That leaves a niche. My mission is to offer people permission to wake up, to fall in love with who you are, to create a daily practice so that you imbibe your greatness. When you say, "YES" to yourself, it's an undeniable feeling because you want that authenticity as much as it wants you. I love quantum transformation – and that is our possibility now – to simply shift.

What you'll be reading next comes from a fun 31 day life experiment I created for myself. By practicing what I wrote, all my dreams came true. I got my creativity, power, heart, passion, joy, balance, trust, love and a millionaire mindset. I invite you to try my experiment and take a turn inward to the mystery that calls you home – home to your heart – home to your soul – home to your divinity...

My business partner and I started our business with $10,000 credit card debt and made millions in 2 years. As of this writing, our business is 6 years old. What a wild whirlwind it's been – full of blessings, gratitude, acceptance, surrender, fear, courage, turmoil, anger, compassion, deep discovery of forgiveness, explorations of greed, generosity, risk, making mistakes, and eventually, the breaking open of my heart.

My main spoken goal 6 years ago was to "master the art of love." Funny how I experienced love and it's opposite – fear knew my first name and had me at "hello." I was too numb to open myself up to intimate love. I couldn't seem to commit. I hid. I was an "entitled victim," you know... my "upbringing screwed me up so how could I be expected to be healthy and fully available?" Can you relate?

I didn't take responsibility for my creation – until I did. However, it was too late for the relationship I was in. Funny, though, how that ending opened me to my new beginning so that I could love. Now love breathes me. My heart is huge. Now love meets love.

I suppose that to master the art of love is to surrender and trust the power within that births planets with a glance, and creates a white burning sun from the heart that stretches galaxies connecting all that to itself. I recognize that inner light in people – we are all connected to Source and are Love.

In this new, young, expressed heart opening, I'm led on a

continuing journey. Ah, the entertainment of it all – from stress, seriousness and struggle, to joy, bliss, and ecstasy – regardless of my circumstances or situations. Now I make up my moments by clearly watching my life as a movie that entertains me, and if it doesn't, I simply make up a new story, circumstance, situation, change out the players...

I believe that you and I are meeting now to simply fall in love more with ourselves. Everything outside of us is just a mirror of the one. In this simplicity, I am. I am you. I am.

So enjoy, splurge, pamper, take care of, love, and adore your lovable self – your worthy self – your perfection. Allow for shifts if anything that is said resonates with you. Perhaps you'll further remember why you are here. Snuggle in with divinity; your heart is the nest that you'll fly from. Embrace the Eternal within and play that experience forward to all. Overcome your fears. You are making them up. They don't really exist.

DAY ONE
THE MADE-UP UNIVERSE OF YOU

A lot of us have more of a fear of being alive then being dead. We fear our greatness. We're taught that we're inadequate – something isn't OK with who we are. So we look outside for some answer, some validation, and we're miserable and don't feel worthy. What if the truth is that everything you've learned is wrong. What if you are worthy as you are? You are perfect as you are. You are vibrantly alive in this present moment. You can live an inspiring Technocolor life. You are one thought away. One thought away from really getting what I'm saying.

Our brain has 100 billion cells. The information in the brain expressed in bits is about 100 trillion bits. If all of this content was written out, it would fill 20 million volumes, which equals the number of books in the world's largest libraries. We have the equivalent of 20 million books inside our heads. What are your thoughts creating? Who is thinking?

A single cell in the human body is doing about 6 trillion

things per second, and it chooses to know what every other cell is doing at the same time. Every cell supports each other, and is nourished by every other cell. The cell is in flow, and the flow is the essence of life. Our cells are more conscious than we are. They know how to support, to be a team. They can depend on each other. They work together in service to the whole. Accept, for now just like your cells already do, that we are are a team exploring the magnificent, grandeur of you. You are safe.

The truth is, all creation is one body, one person, one being, whose cells are connected to one another within a medium called consciousness. We are a miracle. How funny that we would trust the small voice inside that says we are not enough. We are perfection. When you think about all this, how can you not surrender yourself to the creative heart/mind/soul/being/ who orchestrates the universe?

We are pre-disposed to great genius and riches in spite of our small egos telling us we are something other than who we truly are. Recognize yourself; you are wired for greatness. We are souls with egos. What we're going to do together is simply guide the ego toward that inherent, and often forgotten, greatness.

We can treat the part in us that forgets like we would a child who is having a tantrum. Would you beat your kid up, or make her wrong, fearful, or doubtful about how precious she is? No way! Not if you're healthy and supportive, and nurturing... that's all I'm asking you to do for yourself.

Our egos aren't even kids; they're more like crotchety, paranoid, old people who are set in their ways, stuck, and not open to change. We know best, so we think − until we don't; till we wake up to our inner child who lives moment-by-moment in discovery, awe, wonder, fun and imagination, while trusting that all is well. Let's play so we'll stay out of our heads and remain in our smarter hearts, ok?

Read this section again. Fall in love with yourself. Allow your head to get out of the way. I'm talking to the part of you that is really ready and ripe to unlock the fortress of your heart,

48

the part that chooses to be richly filled with a joyous vision of the highest good for all.

To experience yourself as the miracle you are, begin with the words: I AM. Be quiet and still, and when the 'monkey chatter' inside subsides another voice will speak if you listen. It's a voice within that understands and accepts the miracle that is you. Just listen, notice and write about what comes up for you. Who dreams you into form? Explore the mystery of who brings what comes your way. Believe in deliberate co-creation – moment-by-moment awareness of your soul's delight.

DAY TWO
I BELIEVE... I BELIEVE... I BELIEVE

Imagine sucking on a lemon. Do you pucker up? The brain can't tell the difference between what's real and what's imaginary. You can easily make the imaginary, real. Anything you tell yourself – I'm fat, I'm stupid, I'm poor... guess what happens? The subconscious will start to send these messages out then begin to accommodate you.

Imagine the conversation that happens in your head when you think, "I'm fat." Oy, I hate when that happens. OK, what do I do with these thoughts? It's leftover 'think loaf' again. Send in the craving for chocolate, and get too lazy to exercise. Let's eat massive amounts of food. Come here, sugar baby, let me hold you tight. Let's get fat. Misery, disgust, apathy, disappointment, and depression report to the stage. We're enacting the big tragedy again..."

The more you believe it, the more it becomes real. Now turn it around... "I feel healthy, toned, and energized. I feel great about myself." Remember when you puckered up? Was there a real lemon in front of you, or just something you made up that instantly became real?

Fat or healthy? Poor or wealthy? Stupid or smart? What messages do you send to yourself?

Anything you envision, imagine, and focus on can easily

become real. Create it within your sensual mind's heart, and it will be.

The more you believe, the more real it will become.

If what I'm saying is true, then what are you imagining for yourself right now? As a kid you could be the ruler of the universe, talk to fairies, or become stronger then Hercules. Anything was possible. So Superwoman or Superman, what can you choose to believe right now? What makes you super happy? Super evolved? Super aware? Super successful as defined by you or you in love with you?

Anything you clearly envision, imagine, and focus on easily becomes real. This is so. So it is so. Believe it or not...your choice.

Live a life guided by consciousness, not one dictated by the lowest common thoughts most people follow without question. If you are playing a small dream game – there is a selfishness in that – you are here to serve, to share – regardless of risk or what others think of you. Most people don't care much about you – they care about themselves and how they look in comparison with you – still you choose to expand and find people who are secure around your limitless self. You are not choosing to support their insecurity anymore - - interrupt the pattern, and embrace your power.

Most of us are grownup five-year-olds in lipstick or a suit who never doubt or contemplate what and why we believe what we do. Our beliefs are a string of thoughts we got from somewhere or someone; some are like cooties, some are divine, and some are so old they need to be sent home to sleep permanently.

What are your most unhealthy thoughts? Where did they come from? How come you still believe them? Are they right? Why? Do they support you in fully being who you want to BE? Do you feel whole from believing these thoughts? Could you let go of these beliefs now? Why or why not?

Notice any belief you are fighting for, defending, or believing in as your hard, formed, crusty reality that doesn't support you anymore. Just notice. There's nothing to do now. Just check out your beliefs about your core. Love, Intimacy, Money, Fun, Spirit, Health, God… What rules hold you? What do you value? Why?

You can choose to shift right now. Any beliefs that don't fill you up till you're sooooo, sooooo yummy to yourself get to disappear – just like all thoughts. Think about a moose. Where did that moose come from? Eventually that moose will disappear. Thank your beliefs for playing. "Thanks, icky thoughts." "Thanks, destructive, angry, shriveled up little thoughts." "Thanks paranoia." "Thanks depression." "Thanks over-sensitivity." "Thanks negativity." "Thanks anxiety." "Thanks fear." "Thanks judgment and blame."

Say good night to any thoughts or beliefs that don't hold you as a precious source of love. Take the negative ideas and beliefs in deeply, profoundly – breathe them in deeply – have compassion for yourself and all the others who believe what they were told long ago, even though they can't remember the name or face of the person who told them something that all these years is holding them or you back – whatever it is. "Bye-bye – you're not welcome anymore."

Choose new beliefs that are beyond your comfort zone. We come from abundance, possibility, limitless, excitement, passion, courage – are you with me? Right now, we expand our courage and welcome risks. We'll look stupid if that's what it takes to risk. We'll be wrong. Woe's me – we'll be wrong. We've been so attached to being right in the past. We've created war and lost allies, friends, lovers and co-workers, all just to be right. Here's a new belief: I don't need to be right. It's OK to be wrong.

However small or seemingly insignificant your thoughts seem to be, you get to exchange hurt for compassion and transform fear into love. Think of something that hurts you – a person, a situation, a circumstance. Make it current. Come on, something's got your panties or boxers in a twist right now. Something is scaring you right now. What is it? Now is the time to expose it all. Why not? Write it down. This is for you. Write it in invisible ink if you're worried someone will see it.

Cool. So now you're clear about something, or someone who is bugging you. In truth, nothing outside of you can affect you. No one has power over you. No circumstance is bigger than you. Your programming, your values, or your need to make things look a certain way determine what's going on with you. Let's say someone doesn't show up on time, and you feel hurt or disappointed. Clearly, they are not valuing you or your time. Guess what? That's your way of reacting or responding. Someone else might have enjoyed the extra minutes while waiting.

There's no wrong or right, just two different responses or ways to make meaning out of a neutral event. One keeps you happy and at peace, while the other has you suffering. It's always your choice. Love what is because it is.

For fun, envision the same circumstance, a.k.a 'circus stance,' that hurt you and now imagine it as a neutral event. It's not personal. It just is what it is. Before it was a mistake and now it's a lesson. Before it was someone doing something to you. Now you own your power. Before it was unforgivable, based on false beliefs or your need to be right, or to make someone else wrong. Now it's forgivable – you forgive yourself for needing to be right, or creating tension, and you forgive someone else, because in truth, they were doing what they know.

Someone just stole your database. Someone just had an affair. Someone said they don't love you anymore. It's not personal. None of it is. It is what they learned, what's acceptableto them, what comes naturally, what they're working on, what they're ignorant about... They just don't get it yet, or don't agree with your values. See the gift in it now.

So now your fear becomes love. Your hatred becomes forgiveness. Your anxiety is not needed. Your anger is diffused in understanding. You don't need to hold others in such a rigid pattern that they can't breathe and be themselves – flawed, scared, doing their best, spontaneous, sometimes unkind, unaware, not mindful, not perfect according to your definition of "perfect." And that's OK. It's more than OK. It is what is. Just try it on. Like a costume, you can always take it off.

You were a sheeple for so long, believing that you were unlovable, stupid, no good, or a failure. Now sheeple, follow the new flock into transforming those old debilitating, disfiguring plain old, flat out wrong ideas and beliefs about yourself, and know your greatness. Now. Know your greatness now!

Right now, right now, right now, wake up – inhale. This is simple. Inhale deeply and think of all the pain and hurt you've experienced and take in the raw loneliness; the pain of your life not working and all the fear, and not feeling worthy – suck it in – feel it deeply. On your exhale, transform those feelings with the opposite.

Inhale: fear, loneliness, despair – whatever issue is bothering you.

Exhale: transform the 'negative' into it's opposite – fear becomes compassion, for instance.

Now think of all the people on the planet feeling what you feel – all the sorrow and pain and suffering. Feel it, experience it.Then simply let it go on your out-breath so you are free of the pain. With your breath, you will gain deep compassion for all humanity and for yourself.

Just one breath can support you in being new in the world. Don't walk around as another problem – too small to change the world – no, no. Transform yourself. Shift your challenges into gifts, into peace, into love, into compassion. Don't feel it just for yourself, feel it for everyone on the planet. You are never alone. Do you get that? You are never alone. Do this as a mindful, soulful practice and change your life. You are powerful. You are compassionate. You are love.

In a child's mind where the smile spirit lives and bounces, there is the belief that everything is possible; this is where we are beginning our journey. So welcome! Ah, yes, the Smile Spirit has entered your body again… I recognize you now!

DAY 3
I THINK I CAN. I THINK I CAN. I THINK I CAN.

"That which is looked upon by one generation at the apex of human knowledge is often considered an absurdity by the next, and that which is regarded as a superstition in one cen- tury, may form the basis of science for the following one."
– Paracelsus, 16th century mystic and alchemist

We think 60,000 thoughts a day. I don't know who said that. I'm just repeating a supposed fact that made me say, "wow!" out loud. It created such a stir inside that I really chose to ask myself, "What do I think with all those thoughts? How many are really mindless chatter, a stream of complaints, the rantings and ravings of me unconscious, and trivial, a clutter of stuff that doesn't serve anyone? And how many are ones that birth planets, create life, change someone's life, heal, inspire, motivate and activate? How many are the catalyst that becomes the fire, passion and purpose in someone's life? How many are generated from the small voice named, ego? How many are from the being that seems to share my space that is divine and separate from what I call my identity?

These thoughts are tricky flowing things sometimes – think one, you gotta think another. They're like a waterfall, a river, from the source, and then diverted at times or dammed up with one bigger thought. "Hey thoughts, let's be mindful and think these kinds of thoughts a whole bunch, OK?"

It's possible I've found cooperation and honest delight with these thought beings; they love to support and make things come true. These thoughts, the 60,000, are like sculpted fairy dust – the unformed become formed in matter and light.

Thoughts are like magnets; they're the great attracters. They're the great seducers. The great enrollers. Every thought has consciousness and a desire to please. Think of them as genies – your wish is their command. When you say "I am committed to becoming financially free," think of an extremely loud voice saying, "AS YOU WISH!!!!"

How cool is that?! It's handled. Now, imagine saying, "I'm not good with money. I'm always broke." Scream out loud: "AS YOU WISH!!!" Now you get to play the victim. Blame someone, judge someone, point to circumstances.

Darned circumstances... The problem with taking responsibility for your life is that there is no one to blame. C'mon, you genie you – catch a clue – catch a wish. In this story, while we're together they all come true. Remember your power and take responsibility.

From now on – let's pinky swear on this OK? – after every thought you think, say out loud: "As you wish" - Try it. Out loud. It's fun. "As you wish." Now wish for something. Come on. Don't pass up a chance to really take a moment for yourself and just wish for something. Anything. Get out of your head and jump, leap, or fly into your heart. What is your wish? Now say, "As you wish."

This thought will now always follow all your thoughts. Why? Because you're seeing patterns on how you think. Positive or negative. By thinking for a moment, you can witness your thoughts. Just stop and witness your thoughts. How many are serving you? How many are not? It's simple. Once you're trained and mindful, you won't need to say, "As you wish."

I'm sure that at least one of you out there is saying, "Easy for you to say! If you only had my stinky little life you'd know there's no way out... I'm stuck." (As you wish.) Or "I don't have time to create the life of my dreams!" (As you wish.) Ouch, ouch, owie, cancel, cancel – stop that story; it doesn't serve you any more.

What are you focusing on? Listen to your thoughts. What stories do they make up? Are they helping you be powerful? Passionate? Vulnerable? Tender? In love with yourself or not?

Dr. Masaru Emoto did a simple experiment in which he talked to two identical jars of cooked rice every day for one month. At the end of the month, the jar of rice that was told, "thank you," was mildly fermented and had a slight, malted rice smell. The other, which was told daily, "you fool," turned black and rotted. How do you talk to yourself and those around you? This same man is responsible for over 10,000 photographs of frozen water crystals exposed to positive and negative thoughts, words, prayer, music and blessings. Ordinary tap water, negative thoughts, and heavy metal music do not form crystals. They create distorted, ugly and/or sickly shapes. The ones exposed to positive thought, prayer, and beautiful music created extraordinarily gorgeous, sharp, symmetrical shapes.

Water is influenced by energy. Our body is 75+% water. So is our home, Earth. We are influenced by thought and energy. What are you thinking?

DAY 4
WO/MANIFESTATION

Here are some ideas – some mindsets – to gently guide you toward Wo/manifestation. Turn on some inspiring music and quietly contemplate the following:

GREAT ATTITUDES FOR A HEALTHY WAY OF BEING

The premise behind your wishes coming true is simply this: desire, ask, believe and receive. You can make it really hard and suffer a whole lot. You can get addicted to the sad, dramatic, "oh me, oh my story" and pain will be yours. Or just relax and trust. I, not being a masochist, choose the second.

"I myself do nothing. The Holy Spirit accomplishes all through me." – Blake
"Every blade of grass has its angel that bends over it and whispers, "Grow, Grow." – Talmud

In truth, the invisible – the divine – is here with us. There are a lot of beings we can't see, yet we trust somehow that they're with us. They just are. We think we're doing all this stuff to achieve our goals. Meanwhile, they think we're really funny because we live out the human drama with such seriousness.

Ego says, "I, me, mine... aren't I great... look what I did..." This is just a primitive lack of awareness of what I think is so. I may not be correct about all of this, but what if I am? Then 'let go, let God' would be my belief, my way of being.

What if I really believed that I don't do anything? Whew, wheeeeeeeee, that's a big breath of an idea, and it's very reassuring, calming and relaxing. In this case, I bet I'd turn out to be one of those people with lights in my eyes – you know the ones... they have a giggle in their spirit. They're lit from within. There's a grace, a magic, an ease about those who really believe that spirit speaks through them. They are an inspiring expression of spirit.

It is these angels on Earth who are all around us that I'm in love with. They sit on bus benches, in parks, at work. They heal us. They are in love with life. They understand that they're a part of a huge whole. When they're alone they are not lonely. They're not separate.

OK, left brain thinkers, a moment of science again... Darwin said survival depended on eating or be eaten. Win/lose. Strong/weak. It's the ultimate theory to keep us separate. Thankfully, Quantum Physics in the early 20th century proved what ancient sacred texts have been saying for thousands of years: we are not separate from our environment; we are part of an interconnected universe. We literally resonate with our world. Every time you use your toaster, the fields around it perturb charged particles in the farthest galaxies ever so slightly.

Something in us is eternal – matter, electrons, some endless story, intentions. Something in us isn't born and never dies; it is connected to everything and knows everything. From Einstein, it's known as "The Field." In Star Wars they called it, "The Force."

You might ask, "How do I embrace this fully?" For me, it's like the "Groundhog" movie with Bill Murray. I remember who I truly am, and then somehow in the midst of the day, I forget and need to start all over again. My passion and compassion keeps me on a path to remember.

Inside us lives a great being. You are connected to different rules than the ones you're generally told to pay attention to. In the quiet, there is another voice, another sense of who you are that will speak if you are patient and use your imagination. Shhhhhhh, listen to the soul who inspires or guides you. Ask yourself: Who thinks my thoughts? Who listens?

"And now that you've had a good think, stop thinking and talking about it. There is nothing you will not be able to know."
– Zen

"Explore daily the will of God. - Jung
Imagination is more important than knowledge."
– Einstein

"I shut my eyes in order to see. The world of reality has its limits; the world of imagination is boundless."
– Rousseau

"There is no good or bad – only thinking makes it so."
– Shakespeare

To satisfy your ego make up a really good story about how brilliant and right you really are. If you're really smart you'll laugh at yourself, get serious, and then get dumb again. Be too stupid to think. Thinking only gets you into trouble at this stage of the wo/manifestation game.

If you're in truth, in silence, in acceptance, in grace, in divinity, in surrender, in the shhhhhhh of it all, well then, God/spirit tends to talk. And there you are just listening, no strategy, no 'have to,' no shoulds. Just listening and being nothing. There's an opening, a desire to serve the highest good. Then you're able to make a ritual of exploring the will of God through your imagination. You are set free in limitless imagination.

"Life shrinks or expands in proportion to one's courage."
– Anais Nin
(There's a key…find your inner lion. Your adventurer).

"Be really whole and all things will come to you." – Lao-Tsu

It's scrumptious to be whole. Feel your new reality aka free-ality. Experience and create your life's dream in joy and bliss and trust that your limitless prayers are answered.

Just for a second, trust your Self to throw out an idea or two about what you desire. No hesitation. Maybe the old you would stop here, all stuck in your head, needing to be right, to be liked, to be accepted… It's such an old story. Doesn't it seem ridiculous to manifest in a contracted, teeny weenie way when there's so many options that are way more fun? Quick! What's the first thing that comes to your heart that makes you smile out loud?

WHAT I DESIRE IS? (Note, I am laughing out loud)

"Go confidently in the direction of your dreams! Live the life you've imagined. As you simplify your life, the laws of the universe will be simpler." – Thoreau

Desire, ask, believe, receive.

Another way to live the life of your dreams without a lot of struggle is to explore being a time-traveler. Visit the "future" at a time when you have the things you want. You'll be unstoppable if your vision for your "future" is clear. All your thoughts will head out to make it happen. That's their job, and they love it.

As Meister Eckhart says, "When the soul wishes to experience something, she throws an image of the experience out before her and enters into her own image."

How cool is that?! Try it. Enter into your own image. Play there. Get inspired there. It is where you are choosing to live.

What I am discovering is that the childhood song is true: "Life is but a dream…" So dream that you can time-travel into what we understand as the "future." Go there and just Be. In this moment, there is no right or wrong; no "this is stupid," or "I have no time for this." You can create anything you want with your intention.

"The day will come when, after harnessing space, the winds, the tides and gravitation, we shall harness the energies of love. And on that day, for the second time in the history of the world, we shall have discovered fire."
– Teilhard de Chardin, 20th century paleontologist,
Jesuit priest, and philosopher

Discover your fire – your passion – your wahoo! Celebrate and appreciate everything. Live your life as an experiment. Don't know anything. Everything is new, breath by breath. You are perfect as you are. Dream big enough so you birth planets with your laughter. Leave a legacy that inspires so love touches all understanding.

Nothing can contain a soul who is awakened. Wake up. Wake up. Believe 10 impossible things before breakfast. Like Gandhi said, *"Be the change you want to see in the world!"*

You're making your life dream up. It's fleeting and it's not 'real,' so imagine like a child in fun, wonder and awe as you create your inspiring life. I am honored that you made me up so I could tell you this story of "The Little You - You Who Could!"

With great respect and love,

Wendy Robbins

Linda Hollander
"The Wealthy Bag Lady"
Author of *Bags to Riches: 7 Success Secrets for Women in Business*
Founder of the Women's Small Business Expo

Linda Hollander is known as the "Wealthy Bag Lady." Starting out worse than broke – buried in debt and unable to find a way out of the poverty trap, Linda is now the industry leader in teaching entrepreneurial women how to go from Bags to Riches.

In 1988, Linda and her best friend, Sheryl Felice, launched a business called, "The Bag Ladies," in which they sold custom-printed paper and plastic shopping bags to leading-edge companies. Wanting to ensure their success, Linda talked to the nation's top business and financial experts, and searched long and hard for the best method of building a successful business. Ultimately, she decided to create her own success formula.

The sales and marketing plan which she devised made their fledgling business profitable in a very short amount of time, drawing clients such as Disney, Cisco Systems, Mattel, Warner Brothers, Yamaha, Revlon, Ocean Spray, Sears and Nissan. As revenues for the company increased, she had the opportunity to meet thousands of entrepreneurial women. After listening to their stories, she realized that she had the know-how to help them increase their success. So she founded the Women's Small Business Expo, a massive empowerment event which takes place every year.

Linda has over 20 years of business experience. She is a small business consultant, popular international speaker, newspaper columnist and frequent television and radio guest. She is also the author of *Bags to Riches: 7 Success Secrets for Women in Business*. Her powerful success strategies will change your life forever.

Linda lives in Los Angeles, California with her husband, Leslie Greenfield, and their two cats, Carmella and Sneakers.

Free Report: 7 Biggest Business Blunders and How to Avoid Them
www.WomensSmallBusinessExpo.com

Free Quiz: Are You a Natural Entrepreneur?
www.WealthyBagLady.com

Call 866-Women-Biz
Linda@WealthyBagLady.com

The Wealthy Bag Lady's Guide to Success in Your Own Business

By Linda Hollander

My Story

My name is Linda Hollander. I'm known as the "Wealthy Bag Lady." I'll tell you why in a little while, but first let me tell you my story. I own a thriving business in partnership with my best friend, Sheryl Felice. I work as a small-business consultant, speak internationally to groups on business success, and I'm the founder of the Women's Small Business Expo, a massive empowerment event for female entrepreneurs.

If you think I'm a natural businesswoman, think again! Before I started my own business, I was so deeply in debt I didn't know which end was up. For most of my life, I thought business was intimidating, not to mention boring. It was something for men, not for me. I never took one business class in college—all of my college studies were in art. But I've achieved an exciting, successful life through business, and I'm here to help you tap into your female power, so you can do the same.

The Abyss

The lowest point of my life was in 1988. I was worse than broke. I was buried in major debt, and afraid to go to my mailbox because of the bills I couldn't afford to pay. Credit card companies and their lovely debt collectors were constantly harassing me on the phone. I was working like a dog in a dead-end job as a giftware sales representative, and battling the horrendous Los Angeles traffic to get to my office. My bosses were obnoxious, overbearing alpha males from another culture, almost another planet.

I was also living in a low-rent apartment, concealing the whereabouts of my "family"—my beautiful cat, Tuffy—from my landlord, and constantly worried about being discovered. I couldn't afford to live anywhere else.

On the highway of men, I was constantly getting off on the "Jerk Exit," and during that period, I was dating a temperamental and abusive man. He never abused me physically, but he certainly did emotionally. Unfortunately, my self-confidence was so low that I thought this relationship was what I deserved. I couldn't even imagine being in a loving relationship with a man.

Then one day I had an epiphany. I realized I didn't want to be just a part of someone else's plan. I wanted to create my own destiny. I wanted to live my own passionate life, and I wanted to make a contribution. I knew it was time to strike out on my own.

I decided to fire my idiot boss and dump my jerky boyfriend. Then I picked up the phone and called my best friend, Sheryl Felice, who I've known since I was 13 years old. I asked her to go on the biggest adventure ride of our lives together and start a business. Fortunately, she was game.

We started our company, which we called, "The Bag Ladies." We created custom-printed, promotional shopping bags for leading-edge companies, like Disney, Mattel, Cisco Systems, Revlon, Yamaha, Warner Brothers, Sears and Nissan. You've probably seen our bags at trade shows and shopping malls. Because we were one of the only female-owned packaging companies in the country, women entrepreneurs were attracted to our business. I learned about the special issues, challenges, fears and motivations of women entrepreneurs.

Eventually, I started doing small business consultations. One day, a client said to me, "Linda, you're not just a bag lady. You're a Wealthy Bag Lady." I loved it. The name "Wealthy Bag Lady" became my brand identity. I wanted to teach other women entrepreneurial skills so they could become the masters of their own lives.

The next step on my entrepreneurial path was to begin teaching seminars. I could hardly believe that I was getting up and speaking in front of crowds of strangers, but I had so much to share. Much to my amazement, I discovered that public speaking was stimulating, rewarding, and fun.

My next big leap was to create the Women's Small Business Expo, a massive empowerment event where women could be mentored by the nation's top business leaders, form success teams with other women entrepreneurs and have a great time learning about success. From one step to the next to the next—what an exhilarating ride it's been!

And, by the way, right after I dumped the abusive boyfriend, I met a great guy who is a fellow cat-lover and entrepreneur. We are now happily married with two beautiful cats and Leslie is the best man I've ever known.

The Benefits of Being Your Own Boss

My life changed when I went into business for myself. I became fulfilled creatively, financially, and emotionally. Instead of dreading my dead-end job, I flew out of bed in the morning with a kazillion new ideas for my business. Rather than just earning a living, I became the architect of my own life.

You Go, Girl!

Do you own your own business? Are you thinking of starting one? If so, you're in very good company. Women entrepreneurs are the fastest growing segment of the economy. We are starting businesses at twice the rate of men and claiming our true economic power. We are a force to be reckoned with. This isn't just because we've been held back so long—it's because we're good at it. Being a woman is our source of power in business, not our weakness.

Capitalize on your feminine strengths. Some of the most talented business people can read profit and loss statements,

65

but neglect to pay attention to their intuition. Use that famous female sixth sense. If you get a bad feeling about the character of a prospective customer or business associate, heed your body's warning instead of ignoring it. Your first impression is usually right. Listen to your inner voice.

As winning women, we are more likely than men to admit when we don't know something and ask for help. Being natural networkers, we seek out mentors and develop a great supporting cast. Within our companies, employee-management relationships form into supportive teams, rather than hierarchical structures. It is right and desirable to honor your femininity when measuring business success.

Treat your staff like your extended family. Making sure an employee has the time off and the mental clarity to care for a sick child—then seeing that employee productively back at work and the child healthy—is as much a business success as a good quarterly report. In fact, it will probably have a more positive impact on your quarterly report than a man would ever imagine.

Many women believe that true wealth is the ability to run the business from your home and have more time with your family. You can work where you want, when you want. Some women business owners are motivated by freedom, independence and financial rewards. Others are driven by emotional rewards, the need to express their creativity and the desire to make a difference. Opening a day care center may not put you on the cover of Forbes magazine, but it will satisfy your need to shape the lives of the children who will be our leaders of tomorrow.

From the time of birth, as females, we are relationship-oriented. We create powerful bonds and connections. In business, this translates to nurturing clients and providing great customer service. In sales, we are better able to focus on helping others rather than pushing products. We ask poignant questions, learn about our customer's needs, and offer extraordinary solutions. To skyrocket your business, cash in on the feminine.

Becoming an entrepreneur, if you so choose, will take you

into worlds you never imagined inhabiting. You will make decisions about everything from your phone system to the branded image of your company. You will deal with high-level professionals—designers, lawyers, investors—to move your business forward. By meeting challenges and taking risks, you will grow every day and feel truly alive.

Practice lifetime learning. Don't ever become complacent and think that you know it all. Part of your lifetime learning involves investing time and money in yourself without guilt or apology. Finding mentors, attending seminars, reading books, and forming success teams are all a part of the curriculum.

Develop the mindset of a wide-eyed child always eager to learn new things. Each day will bring you new problems to solve, new challenges, new things to learn. I believe every woman should start her own business, even if it's only part time, even if it's just to get a taste of it. Here are just a few of the reasons:

Freedom and Independence

Liberty is so precious to Americans that it's written on every one of our coins. Claim your power. You want it. Go ahead and get it! Freedom and independence are the number one reasons that women start businesses. The true measure of success is being able to live on your own terms. Only then are you able to live your passionate life and do it bravely. When I was an employee, my boss decided on my hours, my salary, and my vacation days. As an entrepreneur, I claimed my freedom and determined my true worth.

Flexibility: Time with Your family

Has your son or daughter been rehearsing for weeks for the school play and wanting you desperately to be there? Does the performance take place during business hours? With your own business, you can rearrange client meetings and work obligations so that you can see your child play a stop sign in the school play.

As the visionary of your company, you can create a family-friendly environment. Your pets can be your furry little office companions. You can take vacations whenever you want. Why confine yourself to the traditional two weeks a year? Even if your business demands long hours when you first get it started, you can choose what hours you work, and keep the rest of your life in perspective.

Financial Potential

Business ownership is the fast track to wealth. In the book, *The Millionaire Next Door*, 99 percent of the millionaires interviewed by authors, Thomas Stanley and William Danko, owned their own businesses. Most of the wealthiest people in the world are entrepreneurs. Oprah Winfrey is a great talk show host, but she is also the CEO of her own company, Harpo Productions. Bill Gates of Microsoft, Ruth Handler of Mattel, and Michael Dell of Dell Computer all rose to mega-wealth through entrepreneurship.

This is not to say that all small businesses succeed. Many don't, and many take years to become profitable. But the fact remains that when you work for someone else, the amount you earn is dictated by your employer. Despite the challenges, the potential for gain is far greater when you work for yourself.

Empowerment

Starting your own business is a passport to self-esteem and empowerment. It is a rite of passage into a kind of adulthood that has nothing to do with age. In many ways, a superior -subordinate relationship with a boss is similar to a parent-child relationship. In a disagreement, you can argue your point, but you have to defer to the authority figure. Just as rebellion is part of growing up in years, you may feel the need as an adult for what psychologists call, "creative rebellion." When you start your own business, you grow into a second adulthood by deciding on the direction of your own life.

Becoming a business owner also gets you into an exclusive club. It's a gutsy move and your reward is to associate with other mavericks who will share their business strategies with you. You will meet them through your business and at industry meetings, conferences, associations, chambers of commerce, and networking functions. Associating with these visionaries is empowering.

Bust Through the Roadblocks

I absolutely believe that as women, we can be hugely effective and find tremendous satisfaction through business. I also acknowledge that we face roadblocks to our success. Recognizing these roadblocks is the first step to breaking through them. Here are some of the most common roadblocks for women:

Fear

In our early childhood, we have no fear of failure or fear of rejection. We want to start walking, so we take a couple of clumsy steps, only to fall flat on our face. But do we quit? No. We just get up again and take some more steps with no thoughts of failure, embarrassment, or looking foolish. We don't worry about people not loving us because we failed. Failure is a part of our learning and growing as a person. We don't get points for playing it safe. Fear wears many different masks: procrastination, perfectionism, and even arrogance. Fear of the unknown is universal. Human beings are creatures of habit and, by nature, afraid of change. Starting your own business is a huge change.

69

Breaking past the roadblock of fear is about breaking out of your comfort zone. The fear of the unknown is so powerful that most people never get out of their comfort zones. Think about it. The thermostat in your home is based on the concept of a comfort zone. When it is too cold, the heat is activated. When it is too hot, the air conditioning comes on. When the thermostat is in its comfort zone, nothing happens.

Naysayers

The media gives us the impression that our dreams are thwarted by gigantic forces outside ourselves, like the state of the economy. In reality, the danger lies much closer at hand. Instead of being your allies, your friends and family may be critical of your entrepreneurial dreams. They aren't trying to throw a wet blanket on your fire because they're cruel. They care about you and they don't want to see you fail or get hurt.

When you announce your intentions to start your own business, your family and friends might greet you with something like, "Don't you know that practically all small businesses fail?" "Don't you know that it's not the right time to start a business?" "Don't you remember what happened to Aunt Sally?"

Going in a new direction requires courage. You must protect your fragile dreams in their early stages. For me, the naysayer was my father. When I started The Bag Ladies, I had a terrible fight with him. He told me that I was "living in a fantasy world. Who was I to think that I could run a business, when the only training I had in college was art classes?" To add insult to injury, he yelled, "You're not qualified to do anything!"

My father is 5 feet 6 inches tall, but to me, he was always larger than life. I love my father dearly and I needed his approval more than anything in the world. I didn't get it. His words were like daggers to me, but I made a decision. I could believe him and take his words to heart, or I could show him that he was wrong. I knew that it was my time to strike out on my own. I built my business and traveled the world. The rift

70

between my father and I lasted for years, and it left a tremendous hole in my heart. My life was great, but I was missing one thing – my father's approval.

When I started teaching small-business success seminars to women, I sent him an audio tape of one of my classes. Then one day, I answered the phone to a gruff, familiar voice. It was my father calling to tell me he was proud of me. He apologized for all the hurtful things he had said in the past. I was filled with so much love that I thought my heart would burst. Now my father and I have a great relationship. We are so close it's embarrassing, and he's my biggest fan.

Determination

What makes a successful woman entrepreneur? Is it talent? Intelligence? What is the mystical ingredient? It's determination. It's that certain little spirit that compels you to stick it out just when you're at your most tired. It's that quality that forces you to persevere, and find the route around that stone wall. It's the immovable stubbornness that will not allow you to cave in when everyone says give up.

Success is 80 percent attitude and only 20 percent strategy. If you think you can't do something, you'll always be right. If you think you can do it, you'll also be right. When the road gets rocky, you can either give up or move forward. Don't be afraid of failure. The failed experiments are no less valuable than the experiments that ultimately prove successful; in fact, you'll usually learn more from your failures than you will from your successes. Successful people have big dreams. Break through all of the false limitations you've placed on yourself and create your vivid vision.

Mentors

Finding a mentor will put you on the fast track to success. Being mentored allows you to tap into the skills and knowledge of visionaries in positions you aspire to attain. Many successful businesspeople have had mentors who believed in them and pushed them to their greatness.

Mentors come in many forms. Some women are lucky enough to find mentors within their own families. My business partner, Sheryl Felice, has an incredible mom with a keen business sense. Over the years, she has offered Sheryl great advice, inspiration, insight, and breakthroughs.

For Patti Regan of the Regan Group, a full service marketing firm, it was her father who told her she could do anything, and helped her build her business by strategizing on how she could get clients.

Other successful entrepreneurs have found their mentors high in the echelons of business. Doug Mellinger, CEO of PRT Group, a global software engineering services company headquartered in New York, didn't start out with a board of advisors, because "I didn't know what a board of advisors was. I needed mentors."

He called the "number one guy at Merrill Lynch," and kept calling for months until he got an appointment. When the meeting finally took place, Mellinger simply asked the man at Merrill Lynch to be his mentor, requesting that they meet every six to eight weeks so he could ask for advice and get feedback. The man was flattered by the request, and was impressed by Mellinger's persistence. He said, "Sure!" Today, PRT has approximately nine hundred employees and eleven locations worldwide.

Networking Power

Every time you meet someone who might need your goods or services—or even someone who knows someone who fits that description—you have an opportunity to network. Stay alert for great ways to network spontaneously, and also actively seek out networking opportunities. When you first start your business, consider joining at least two organizations, one that focuses on your chosen field, and the other, a more general organization such as a local businesswomen's group.

Going into a room of complete strangers, meeting them one or two at a time, and telling them about you and your business can be even scarier than public speaking, but networking events offer such great bonuses – from mentors to clients – that it's really worth breaking through your fear and shyness.

Tips for Successful Networking

Your first step for successful networking is to walk up to an approachable person, make eye contact, and smile. Your smile is your welcome sign. Introduce yourself with your name, company, and elevator speech.

Always carry plenty of business cards. This advice may seem obvious, but I've met plenty of business people at networking events who didn't even bring their business cards. If possible, wear an outfit with pockets. Keep your business cards in your left pocket. When you reach out your right hand to shake theirs, reach your left hand into the left pocket, pull out a business card and hand it to them. Put the business cards you collect at the event in your right pocket.

Don't be stingy about those business cards! Recently I met a great promoter, DeLyn Patrick of DLP Career Coaching. When we exchanged cards, she didn't just give me one of her business cards, she forked over a whole stack so that I could pass them out to friends and associates. Smart lady!

Here are some other strategies for effective networking:

Get to the event early. The front tables at events tend to be "power tables." By arriving early, you can assure yourself a seat in these influential circles. If there is a speaker, you can Also claim a prime seat to see the speaker without the obstructions of big heads and hairdos. In addition, getting there early will ease any nervousness you may be feeling.

Give, then receive. Resist the temptation to over-promote. Instead of giving a long commercial about your business, introduce yourself briefly. Then ask the other person, "What can I do to help you?" Really listen to their needs and offer solutions. Invariably, the other person will turn around and ask how they can help you. This turns networking into a two-way exchange where amazing things can happen.

Concentrate on quality, not quantity. According to Jacqueline Jones, former Southwest Regional Coordinator of the National Association of Female Executives, for most people the number of business cards they collect becomes the barometer of their networking success. Instead of just collecting business cards, concentrate on the quality of the contacts you are making.

Take notes. On the back of each card, jot down the date, event, and any important information about that person or their company. Linda Clemons, founder of Sisterpreneur, makes notes about personal information such as birthday, anniversary, children's graduations, etc. Then she calls the person to wish them a happy birthday. She says it's wonderful to hear the surprise and joy in their voice.

Work the room counterclockwise. Most networkers traverse the room in a clockwise manner. To stand out from the crowd, take the road less traveled and go counterclockwise.

Break into conversation circles. This is probably the most intimidating part about networking. It's best to break into groups of three or more people. If two people are talking, they may be discussing something personal or conducting business. Plant yourself near the group so that you can hear what they're talking about. Then position yourself in the group, introduce yourself, and add a comment that relates to the topic being discussed. You can also compliment something a person is wearing or remark on his or her keen insights, intelligence, or storytelling. Everyone loves compliments.

Make eye contact with everyone in the circle. At a recent networking event, I was having a conversation with a man named Bill when Bill's friend Steve came over and joined us. Steve talked only to Bill and never even looked at me. Was I invisible? After Steve left, Bill apologized for his friend's boorish behavior, explaining that Steve was probably shy and uncomfortable. I didn't buy it. You cannot disguise shyness with rudeness. If you're talking to a group of people, make sure you introduce yourself and make eye contact with everyone in the group, not just a select few. Even if you're lucky enough to meet a "make it happen" person, don't ignore his or her associate. If you're talking to a husband and wife, make sure to look at both of them.

Follow up. Write quick emails to the people you met at the event. Call the key influencers to see if you can arrange a meeting. Send thank-you cards and e-greetings to acknowledge a person's importance and make them feel special.

Don't be afraid to network. It's a great way to meet interesting people, broaden your knowledge, and help your business grow.

Success Teams

After you've done your power networking and made some great connections with other visionaries, you'll want to form your success teams. A success team is your hand-picked group of cheerleaders – people who gather at regular intervals to help you achieve your goals.

Being with successful people who have confidence in you and who are actively supporting your goals instills tremendous confidence and initiative. The group intelligence activates imagination and creative energy. The members of your success team also balance out your strengths, weaknesses, experience, and expertise, and widen your horizons.

When I first came up with the idea for the Women's Small Business Expo, the first people I ran it past were the members of my success team. They were encouraging, straightforward, and wonderful. They told me about the holes in my idea and asked me some really important questions that I hadn't even considered.

Effective success team members are straight shooters. Everyone respects the others' ideas, but they don't give rubber-stamp approval to everything that's presented. They challenge you and inspire you, as you do them.

If you capitalize on your inborn female talent for creating relationships, becoming an entrepreneur won't be a one-woman show. An entire cast is waiting to support you as you create your vivid vision, and then move through the adventure of your business life.

Success Team Benefits

The benefits of success teams are myriad. You will tap into the resources, skills, and knowledge of the other members. The group intelligence of your team will help you accelerate your goal attainment, giving you a fresh perspective on projects that you are extremely close to. Synergy is created when the whole is greater than the sum of its parts. You'll be amazed by the degree to which a success team works on a synergy level to inspire breakthroughs. Here are some other benefits of success teams:

Problem solving. Success teams will help you find solutions to your challenges. According to Albert Einstein, "Problems cannot be solved at the same level of consciousness that created them." With the group intelligence you can tap into resources, develop ideas, gain feedback, and bring forth your brilliance.

Confidentiality. The success team gives you a safe forum to share your dreams, goals, and desires. In order to keep the members protected, confidentiality must be respected. What is said in the group stays there.

Banishment of entrepreneurial isolation. At times, business owners operate in a vacuum. This is espcially true if you are running a home-based business. Success teams offer a marvelous opportunity to meet with other individuals of like mind.

Dynamic brainstorming sessions. There's no better place to brainstorm than with your success team. Marvelous ideas and solutions emerge from these brainstorming sessions.

Accountability to yourself and others. People tend to let themselves down before they would let down their esteemed colleagues. The accountability factor is a tremendous force in moving members of the success team along their path toward their goals.

Strong relationships. Even if the success team starts out with the goal of fast-tracking business accomplishments, you will become friends with your group members. An incredible bond is created when harmony of purpose exists.

Forming Dynamic Success Teams

You may want to form more than one success team for achieving a variety of goals. One team might help you with financial issues, another with creative issues. In Corporate America, boards of directors and advisory boards are formalized success teams. These brain trusts spurred the meteoric success of leading-edge companies such as Disney, General Electric and IBM.

I've been on success teams with people I've never met in person. We just talk on the phone at regular intervals. Many people prefer to meet with their success team partners in person, which helps strengthen the bond and achievements.

During meetings, success team members share their accomplishments on their goals from the last meeting, state their new goals, and say what they need help and support with from the group. If you have a project, such as a business plan or marketing piece that needs time for review, you can send it to the group members in advance of the meeting. The quality of the input tends to be higher when people have time to evaluate your project and write down their suggestions in advance.

Here are some additional tips for creating success teams that live up to their full potential:

Name your success team. The name should reflect the common interests, goals, or values of the group.

Create a purpose statement. One of the best ways to run a success team is to develop a group purpose statement that is read at the beginning of each meeting. The purpose statement will be constantly growing and evolving according to the visions of the group members. Here is an example: "Our Purpose: to help each member get more focus in less time, more growth with less effort, and more profits with less stress. By elevating and stimulating the minds of each member, we will all live well, have fun, and help each other achieve personal success by transforming other people's lives. The team members will give first, then receive. Each success team partner understands that the power of the group is greater than the sum of its parts. All members of the success team will be encouraged to be their highest and best selves."

Limit the number of members. Four to six people is a good number for a success team. If your group has dramatic results, word will spread and others will want to join, but it's best to keep the group small so everyone gets a fair share of personal attention and brainstorming.

Qualify your members. New success team members could be nominated by someone in the group, then voted on by the other members. Or you could ask prospective members to write their individual mission statements and tell what they will bring to the group. People have a greater respect for groups if they have to do some work to join them.

Meet regularly. Whether you meet weekly, biweekly, or monthly, regular meeting dates will give the group a sense of structure. One to two hours is a good length for success-team meetings. Be respectful of time differences if you meet by phone from opposite sides of the country.

Assign a team leader. Meetings run more smoothly when someone moderates. The leader reads the purpose statement, monitors each person's contributions so that nobody monopolizes, assigns action items for the next meeting, and wraps up the session with a conclusion. To create a sense of fairness, rotate the role of team leader, either every meeting or every few meetings.

Make use of a "hot seat." One of the great benefits of a success team is assistance on specific projects. The person who gets her project reviewed is in the hot seat. To be fair to the other members of the group, rotate the hot seat so that everyone gets the advantage of the group dynamic.

Five-Star Customer Service

The nurturing of relationships is the vanguard of women. In married couples, it's usually the woman who maintains the relationships with friends and family and schedules the get-togethers. Following up with your customers is the key to maintaining your crucial business relationships.Five-star customer service entails far more than just filling orders and responding to inquiries and complaints. It's all about showing that you care. People don't buy from faceless companies. They buy from people. Your customers want a human relationship with you, not just a business relationship. They want to trust you, be respected by you, and feel good about doing business with you. Do everything you can to strengthen your relationship with your customers, for their sakes and for yours.

Great companies view customer service as a profit center rather then an expense, because serving your customers' needs creates profit. Strive to consistently deliver a level of service that exceeds and even anticipates the customer's expectations and provides experiences that show you care. There is always something extra you can do that will give you the unfair advantage in business and set you ahead of the pack.

Show Your Appreciation

There are many ways to show your appreciation to your customers, and one of the best is with handwritten notes. This is where women can really excel in business relationships. In the technological age, the art of the handwritten thank-you note has become lost. Handwritten notes are personal and win hands down over form letters. Folks remember a caring person who took the time to write a personal note. The thank-you card may even be displayed in the customer's home or business.

Don't buy generic thank-you cards from the store. Make your own personalized cards branded with your company name. You can buy greeting card paper at the office supply store and print them on your color printer, or you can order them from an office supply catalog. Either way, be sure to hand-write a personalized message.

The internet has helped automate the process of thanking clients. If someone places an order on your web site, have an autoresponder email send them a thank you. Email is also good for jotting quick notes of appreciation to customers and colleagues.

You don't have to spend a fortune to show you care. A simple gesture on your part will keep them placing orders, and referring new customers.

Stay in Touch

Your fortune is in your follow-up. A key ingredient of your customer follow-up is to have ongoing communication. Call from time to time, not necessarily to get the next order or referral, but just to see how the customer is doing. Send e-mail announcements of upcoming specials and solutions for your customer's business.

Share information you think might be useful, recommend a good book, forward a relevant newspaper article. Women are masters at this.

A newsletter is another marvelous way to stay in touch with your regular customers. It could be a simple one-page sheet, a fancy newspaper-type document, or an e-mail correspondence. The newsletter could contain updates of company operations, news about the customers themselves, and information about new products and services. Be sure to include customer testimonials.

In addition, send your customers cards for birthdays, anniversaries, and holidays. These friendly greetings will ensure that your business remains in your customer's mind.

The more committed you are to keeping your customers loyal, the faster your company will grow.

Be the Hero of Your Own Life

At some time, we've all had a dream of how our life could be, but our dreams got buried in the everyday frustrations of life. Most people feel that the events of the world control them. They get caught up in making a living rather than designing a life.

A study quoted on NBC says that half the people in the United States feel that the only way they can get ahead financially is to win the lottery. The chance of getting hit by lightning is 900 times greater than winning the lottery.

We live in the greatest country in the world, surrounded by opportunities for success at every turn. Yet most Americans are too stuck in their ruts to try something new. To succeed in life, you have to forget about most people. If you want to rise to the top, you have to disregard the opinions, reactions, and warnings of others. You need to believe deep down in your soul that you can run a successful business. Wealth and success come to those who live their lives passionately and bravely.

Value People More than Money

The heart weighs more than the wallet. Your heart carries so much more value than your bank account ever could. It's an extraordinary organ, the origin of your life and your love. Listen to your heart. Connecting deeply with the people we love makes the tapestry of life a rich one. Taking time for others gives us priceless psychological and emotional rewards. Read to your child, share some meaningful conversation with your teenager, have a date with your husband, call a friend and invite her to lunch, rent "chick flicks" and make margaritas for a girls-only night.

Your family and friends are not an interruption to your success journey—they are your touchstones and your reason for being.

Honor the people in your life in small ways whenever you can. Think about the people you love, the business people you admire, your loyal employees, and your favorite customers. Call them when you think of them. Give them gifts. Take them to lunch and acknowledge their special qualities. Tell them about the traits that you admire in them and how much they mean to you.

Give Back to Others

Perhaps the most powerful way to be the hero of your own life is to be a hero to others. Your ultimate task as a hero is to bring knowledge, energy, and power back to the people you love and share it with them. In discovering your greatness and cultivating your inborn talents to share with the world, you can make your contribution and fulfill your mission. You can help those you love and help the society we live in.

Building a successful business is the ultimate opportunity for creating a glorious legacy. Maybe your dreams are global, fighting against evils such as domestic violence and child abuse, or maybe you desire to make life better for the people you love. Your aspirations could lead you to buy a home for your parents, or help out a favorite family member or friend. You could be the one in your inner circle who has the financial ability to say, "Don't worry, I'll take care of it."

Build your business with all your heart. Give power to your compassion. Value people more than money and dedicate yourself to giving back.

Your Life's Story

Go out and write your life's story. As the young Anne Frank said, "How wonderful it is that nobody need wait a single moment before starting to improve the world." Improve your world. Be the hero of your own life.

Get out there and build your successful business. Live your passionate life and do it bravely. Make your contribution and give back to humanity. Discover your greatness. Get out and let your light shine for the whole world. I'll be waiting to hear your story…

Melanie Benson Strick
Founder and President
Success Connections™
The Entrepreneur's Success Coach,
Author and Speaker

Melanie Benson Strick coaches entrepreneurs to align their power and passion to generate profits. She founded Success Connections after more than a decade of work in corporate settings. Realizing that true success doesn't just happen by chance, Melanie saw a need in the workforce for people to receive specialized training, not only in running a small business, but also towards the development and achievement of their life goals.

Through Success Connections, Melanie offers private mentoring, leadership coaching, keynote presentations and seminars. Success Connections' signature programs include Empowered for Life™ and The Power Threshold™, which enables individuals to map out strategies for maximizing results.

In 2004, Melanie achieved Master Certification in Neuro-Linguistic Programming and Hypnosis. She has a Master's Degree in Organizational Management, and is a Coach U Graduate in both professional and personal coaching. She has accreditation in the Insights Discovery System™, and a Bachelors of Science in Business Management. In addition, she is a licensed Spiritual Counselor.

In 2003, she successfully launched the Los Angeles chapter of the Shared Vision Network, and served as President of the International Coach Federation Los Angeles. In 2004, she co-chaired the Small Business Coaching Task Force for the International Coach Federation. Melanie was nominated in 2003 for the 40 Under 40 Award in the San Fernando Valley. The annual award acknowledges significant business growth, visionary leadership and making a difference in the world.

For more information:

Success Connections
877.830.3139
www.SuccessConnections.com

The Power Threshold™: Seven Steps to Leverage Your Personal Power for Greater Freedom and Wealth

By Melanie Benson Strick

"Put yourself in a state of mind where you say to yourself, 'Here is an opportunity for me to celebrate like never before, my own power, my own ability to get myself to do whatever is necessary.' "
Martin Luther King, Jr.

How would you like to spend every day doing what you love? What if you knew that leveraging your personal power would lead to more freedom and wealth? Would it be of value to you to learn seven steps to transform the way you do business – from overwhelm and frustration to clarity and greater success? I thought you might say "yes."

Entrepreneurism is flourishing in our world today. As corporate America loses its reputation as a stable, life-long career path, people are leaving the workforce in droves to start their own companies. Yet on average, a small business will stay open two to five years, and many take as long as ten years to actually turn a profit.

Michael Gerber, the author of E-Myth Revisited, suggests that many entrepreneurs start a business with the best of intentions for freedom, but soon find themselves in "just another job" for themselves, having had no idea of what it really takes to maintain a profitable business.

Having spent the last four years immersed in the small business community, I've seen many types of businesses, from thriving multi-million dollar ventures to struggling private practices. What makes the difference? Why do some business owners thrive while others continually run into blocks and frustration?

For starters, many entrepreneurs operate outside of their "zone of power" or what I call, The Power Threshold™. How do you know if you are not in "the zone?" Review the statements below and see how many apply to you:

❑ Of course I can do it, Ms. Client. Let's see. I can fit it in between 3 a.m. and 3:30 a.m. tomorrow.

❑ Why did I sign up for that _____? (fill in the blank) I barely have enough time to see my kids at night.

❑ Hmmm. I haven't had a real vacation in over a year. Well, I can't start now – I've got too much to do.

❑ Wow, I've got a great idea for a new product/service. I know I haven't finished any of the others I've already got on my plate but this one is much better.

❑ I couldn't possibly have someone help me. I don't have time to train someone and I certainly could never trust anyone to do it as well as I do.

❑ I feel like I'm spinning in circles. No matter how hard I try I just can't figure out how to take these great ideas and make money in a business.

❑ I am so overwhelmed! I can't even think straight, let alone take time for lunch today. How will I ever get all of this done?

❑ I am so bored! Today is absolutely a "computer solitaire" day.

❏ It seems like I'm always busy and working hard, but I never have enough money to pay my bills.

❏ Why did I ever start this business in the first place? Nothing excites me anymore – not my clients, my projects or the company. I used to LOVE this work.

❏ I want to run away to Tahiti, live on the beach, and have a "simple life."

Do any of these statements sound familiar? If you answered yes to at least two of these statements, it is highly likely that you are operating outside of your Power Threshold™. What is the Power Threshold™? The Power Threshold™ is where Power, Passion and Profits align. A Power Threshold™ is an entrance or zone that can be crossed over. When you are in your Power Threshold™, you are "in the zone" – it's where your efforts are in the flow; you are in the groove, having fun, working with great people, and creating boundless wealth. Does doing business in the Power Threshold™ sound good to you? In this chapter, I'm going to share with you a seven-step process that I learned in the school of hard knocks that will allow you to focus your time and resources on results that are fun and lucrative. My own experience of operating outside of my Power Threshold™ has helped me support others in finding theirs. But before I share the details on how you can identify your Power Threshold™, I'd like to share a little bit about why it's important.

My Story

My name is Melanie Benson Strick. I'm just like any entrepreneur – I have a passion for freedom and wealth, and I'm highly motivated, crave creative adventures, and love helping other business owners connect with success. I run a company called Success Connections, a resource center for entrepreneurs and service professionals to help them align their passion, power, profits. In essence, the Success Connections' team mentors people in achieving personal and professional excellence in their small business endeavors.

At this time in my life I actually run two businesses (I'm also the Director for Shared Vision Network in Los Angeles) and serve as co-chair for the International Coach Federation's Small Business Task Force. People ask me all the time "how do you do it all?" It can be a tricky balancing act and I haven't always been good at it.

After one year in business I found myself continually asking, "Why is this so damn hard?" I thought corporate life was tough. I had worked for a major Fortune 500 company for 10 years. While in college I worked for three other major corporations learning "the ropes." During my post-college years I did everything that a good college graduate does – I worked for a prestigious company, began climbing the corporate ladder, learned to play golf and networked with my business associates. I even attained my Master's degree in Organizational Management, but I found myself increasingly disillusioned.

After ten years, I had endured enough of the corporate life. I was tired of corporate politics, trying to figure out how to break through the plaster-board ceiling (I had not even reached the glass ceiling yet!) and I felt trapped.

When things aren't right in my life I go on a quest. Through much reading and researching, I realized that there was this whole other world of "entrepreneurism." I figured since I craved freedom and independence, I must be one, since I fit the description perfectly. Every two years I was restless for new and different roles in the company. Everyone I worked with thought I was undisciplined and difficult to manage (I now understand a key trait of being an entrepreneur is being highly unemployable.)

One day I went to a seminar and I vividly remember a woman saying, "over the next five years, more people will be

90

self-employed." It was almost like a sign. And then it happened. I saw a book by Cheryl Richardson called, Take Time for Your Life. The book talked about what it was like when you actually had time for more than just work. Richardson was a life coach and there was something infinitely appealing about that idea. I immediately hired a coach.

One year later, after much consternation, planning and prodding by my coach, I took the leap into owning my own business. My co-workers thought I was crazy to leave a lucrative job with such a promising future. The only other people we knew "who left" fell into a black abyss (like in the book, Clan of the Cave Bear, when the main character is cast out of the clan and is never heard from again.)

I knew that owning my own business was my only hope at sanity and survival, and hopefully, life fulfillment. Except that, interestingly enough, one year later I was still working as hard as I ever did in my full-time career. I would stay up late every night working on my website, marketing materials, writing newsletters, and doing all the stuff you are supposed to do. I was also giving lots of presentations, and getting involved in every possible networking group and visibility opportunity I could find. I knew that if I could just accomplish being "known," then I would have more revenue, prestige, and clients, and my life would embody the freedom I craved.

But there was always something else I had to accomplish before I could make enough money. What was the secret? Was I alone in this challenge? Did anyone ever really succeed at this small business stuff? Little did I know that the answer was right in front of me.

Identifying The Power Threshold™

The first three steps to Freedom and Wealth as an entrepreneur lie in identifying your Power Threshold™.

Step one is to know what your Power Threshold™ is by identifying the number of hours you want to work and the optimum number of roles/projects that you can take. For instance, you may wear four or five different hats in your business. We all know innately how many different types of projects we can handle and still thrive. One too many and we are in overwhelm. One too few and we tend to get lazy and are under-challenged.

Your Power Threshold™ might look something like this: I work 50 hours per week. I can have 15 active clients (one hour per week each), 2 new products in planning, and 1 outside committee or volunteer role.

Action: Pay attention to how many hours you work, and how many roles or projects you take on. Is there a point when you know that you are in "the zone?" Is there a Threshold™ you cross when you become less effective? Create your Power Threshold™ formula and post it in your office.

Step two is to fully align with passion. Passion is present when our vision of success motivates and inspires us. In the Power Threshold™, your vision of success is present in the type of client you work with. Each of us knows when we have chemistry and magic with a client. If it is not there, your performance will be off. If you find you don't work with clients, translate it to whatever part of the business you connect with.

Action: Create an "ideal client" vision statement. Know exactly who they are, what work you do with them, and how much they pay you. Post it with your Power Threshold™ for - mula.

Step three is to focus on what generates a profit first. Sometimes our passion and enthusiasm takes us off track. When you are in the Power Threshold™, 20% of your effort should be generating 80% of your profit. If you are putting more than 20% effort into something, why? Where is the payoff? I have learned that most entrepreneurs just love to create. And that is OK as long as you don't care about the financial results.

But when wealth is important (and please say it is), then you have to be aware of how you spend your time and what the financial return on your investment is in the end.

Action: Write out how much revenue you desire per month (or per year.) Also write how many hours you desire to work, the number of clients/projects you are working with, and the prices for your product/service – what is your income? Pay attention to your ROI (return on investment.) Focus more of your energy on the highest ROI activities.

How We Found Sandra's Power Threshold™

Sandra is a talented web designer whose business revenue had taken a dive. When Sandra came to me for coaching, she was not generating enough business revenue and her clients didn't give many referrals. As she explained her situation, I found that she routinely was over-committing and under-performing on her web design projects, even though they were a significant part of her income. She was busy 12+ hours a day, however, her financial picture was falling far short of what she desired. I also noticed that Sandra quite often under-quoted her projects just to get the job. Eventually, the project would take many more hours than planned, resulting in diminishing ROI (return on investment.)

Sandra had been exposed at a very early age to all of the motivational gurus so she understood what success was all about, but for some reason it stayed elusive and unattainable, seeming to be light years away from her bank account.

As Sandra and I discussed this interesting paradox, we began to discover that she took on a lot of web design clients just because she needed the money – but she didn't really get a lot of joy in working with them; the projects were either under-stimulating or the clients were excruciatingly difficult to work with.

Upon further exploration, I found out that Sandra had many different types of projects and new ideas that were brewing simultaneously. Her new ideas always seemed to take precedence over the web design projects. The picture that came to mind was one of an ostrich with its head in the sand. Sandra talked about these "other projects" as if they magically happened, without allocating for the time they would take out of her schedule. It was almost as if she didn't realize that just because the project was for her own company that it was actually going to take some time to implement.

At that moment the light bulb went off in my head. The Power Threshold™ concept was born!

Entrepreneurs are at their greatest when they maintain a zone of *power* – when the number of profitable projects they are committed to, and the inspiration and motivation to work on them, is in perfect balance. The Power Threshold™ can be attained when a person has the ideal number of projects, feels passion and excitement for the client/s and the work, and significant profit is generated. One extra project and the scales tip too far and one's motivation hits the floor.

A client who stresses you out, or who is not ideal, turns powerful projects into procrastinated projects. Too few exciting projects and the entrepreneurial spirit is under-challenged and we end up in front of the TV from a lack of stimulation. With a difficult client or a less-than-desirable payment for services, the procrastination button is set on high.

My entrepreneurial, creative, systems-thinking mind lit up and shouted – "What if this was the missing link? What if every entrepreneur knew exactly what their Power Threshold™ formula was? Maybe their ability to focus, plan and create results would double or even triple!"

I ran my theory by a few clients and fellow entrepreneurs and they loved it. Sandra and I identified her Power Threshold™ formula — knowing exactly who her ideal client was, and knowing how many hours she wanted to work, she could take on a certain number of projects at any given time and be in her power.

The Power Threshold™ formula looks like this:

Ideal Client + Stimulating Project + Ideal Number of Projects + Ideal Profit = The Power Threshold™

After realizing how I could help other entrepreneurs with this process, another big light bulb went off – I have to live this, too! I set out to align my own business practices with the Power Threshold™. By this point, I had successfully leveraged myself for the sake of visibility and service by "giving myself away" in too many places. I was in charge of a mastermind program at my church; I was President of the International Coach Federation in Los Angeles; I was being interviewed to start a professional networking organization, Shared Vision Network, in Los Angeles; I had my own coaching business to run; I was finishing two training programs; and I continued to have a plethora of exciting ideas planting themselves in my brain on a daily basis.

I had to "clean up my own house." In doing so, I realized how powerful this concept truly was. Not only was my effectiveness noticeable and my revenue increasing by applying the Power Threshold™, but every one of my clients was having a breakthrough in his or her business as well.

However, I realized there was another dimension to truly achieving personal and professional mastery using The Power Threshold™. It was one thing to identify "the zone" and it would be still another to master it.

What to Do When You Are Out of "The Zone"

Once we identified "the zone" and knew what The Power Threshold™ was, it was easier to know when someone was out of the zone. Through noticing my own patterns and those of my clients, I found that there are two ways in which people get out of "the zone." People who are "above the zone" are great visionaries, however they lack focus and the ability to leverage themselves effectively. These entrepreneurs are amazing at creating new ideas and projects, but have little success at implementing them. They often over-commit and under-perform in their lives and for their clients. Even though they have a comfortable revenue stream, they limit their financial success by over-committing their most precious resource – themselves.

Conversely, people who are "below the zone" lack the proper foundational structure to move forward and are often confused about their vision. They can't seem to generate monetary results from their ideas and passions. People below the zone commit themselves to ideas and projects that produce very little return on investment. People here either have too much financial comfort (i.e. lawsuits, an inheritance or good investments) or lack financial security completely. People who operate "below the zone" seem to go in circles – and always have a reason or excuse for their lack of momentum.

Both groups consistently **get in their own way** — propelling themselves into confusion and disappointment, which results in diminished profits, reduced client activity, and overall frustration with their businesses.

Sandra realized that she spent too much time bouncing above and below her Power Threshold™. Yet she continued to focus her efforts on things other than her web design clients. One of Sandra's "other projects" was writing a book. Every waking hour, she passionately worked with her partner on it. They spent many a day burning the midnight oil, and often her client deliverables slipped by one day, two days, or even a week.

It was obvious that Sandra's greatest love was writing this book. However, in passion for writing this book she was almost blind to her client responsibilities. When a client would become unhappy with her performance, she would push herself to work on the project. I knew that she had passion – but it didn't seem to be directed toward the area of her business that was generating revenue. As we began to apply some "refining tools" to her business, Sandra had more insight into how to master her Power Threshold™.

Mastering The Power Threshold™

Once you have identified your Power Threshold™, in time you will find that it needs to be tweaked and refined to truly reap the benefits. I have found that success and mastery in business (and in life) are about choice – what do we choose to do when faced with distractions and competing needs for our attention? Viktor Frankl, a Nazi camp survivor, once said that every hour of every day there are choices to make whether or not to submit to powers, which could rob your inner being. The choice that you make determines your freedom, and whether or not you "become a plaything of circumstance."

Mastering you Power Threshold™ consists of the next three steps: Time Mastery™, systems and teams. How many times have you closed up your office on Friday afternoon, shaking your head saying, "where did this week go?" Or how about that important goal you set for yourself? Have you ever found yourself looking back after three months and realizing that not only have you not accomplished it, but you have completely forgotten it?!

Step four is Time Mastery™. It seems everyone I know has read a Stephen Covey book on time management or has taken a time management class. But do they have Time Mastery? Not usually, although once in a while someone will surprise me. I coach every client through the process of determining if where they spend their time is in alignment with their Power Threshold™. The Time Mastery™ system helps a person get clear on how much time they truly spend on tasks so they can make informed choices about how to reallocate their time to be in alignment with their vision and priorities.

Action: get clarity on how you spend your time. What per-centage do you spend on the most important tasks and activities?

Step five is systems. Have you every found yourself recreating the wheel? Or maybe you noticed that you were conducting a business transaction and left out a step. I have a friend who was ready to delegate some tasks last year. However, he realized after he hired his assistant that he had to create the systems of how things were done in order to delegate more effectively. I've studied entrepreneurial millionaires and one thing they all have in common is that they can duplicate themselves with the use of systems.

T. Harv Ecker, founder of Peak Potentials and the Millionaire Mind Intensive, says that, "One of the fastest ways to wealth is to systemize your business." Michael Gerber, who is best known for his entrepreneurial systems work, has often said that: "the system runs the business. The people run the system."

I have found in working with my clients that systems must be created to reflect the unique aspects of your business – so don't expect to use a cookie-cutter approach. Feel free to check out the resources page of my website for systems resources.

Action: Create systems to streamline your efforts. What area of your business could be done more effectively with a system? If you were going on a month long vacation, what would you need someone else to know to effectively run your business? Use checklists, flow charts or process maps to create a system for everything you do in your business.

Step six is leverage teams. What could happen in your business if you could leverage the power of other people's strengths, passion and time? Are you an entrepreneur who is a lone wolf, but who secretly craves the collaborative energy of working with others? Leveraging a team is one of the most significant steps an entrepreneur can make. That might mean hiring an assistant to handle the administrative (and often mundane) tasks, or a full staff to handle all of the functions of your business.

As the leader, your vision and creative energy is vital. As many leadership experts will tell you, there is a significant difference between management and leadership. Leaders cast the vision and inspire their teams. Managers implement the vision and ensure the systems are running properly. Both functions must be present to have balance, momentum and strength. Let me tell you from first hand experience, it is not always easy to be a leader and a manager. Creating a strong team can take your business from mediocrity to phenomenal success.

Action: Challenge yourself to start building your team. Pick something that will add significant value to the bottom line and allow you to focus on what you do best. A good place to start might be to outsource your bookkeeping, hire an assistant for emails, phone calls and schedule management, utilize an inter - net marketing assistant, or even hire out your cold calls and sales tracking.

Sandra Masters the Power Threshold™

Once we had identified Sandra's Power Threshold™, she began to understand how her passion was out of alignment with the projects she took on. As she looked at how much time she spent on her book project, she began to see that there was truly very little time left to work on her web design. So we created a "time budget," where she committed a certain number of hours per week to working on the web design (for fun, well-paying clients), then the rest she could allocate to her book project and other "fun" ideas she wanted to pursue.

The next step was to create a streamlined system to handle the start up of a new client and to delegate the programming to her newly established team. By creating a system for how the process flowed from start to finish, details were managed perfectly, the clients were happier, and the projects were completed faster. Sandra's payoff was that by delegating efficiently, she had more time to invest in marketing her new book!

Going Beyond the Power Threshold™

After I began to master my Power Threshold™, I realized that there was another dimension of power. As my clients used the tools to master their Power Threshold™, we found there was always another level of excellence that needed attention along the way. I've realized after years of coaching others that integrating a new skill takes time. It is like learning to ride a bike. First you must learn the principles of how to do it. Then you must practice it. After a while, the body has cellular-level memory of how to ride a bike without even being conscious of it. Step Seven is when new habits and skills become integrated into our being – it is just who we are.

Step seven is the power of excellence. Every day I make a choice to use this system or not. On the days that I don't, I typically won't accomplish much. I will often feel overwhelmed, stressed and burned out. When I do make the choice to use this system, however, I'm unstoppable! Those are the days that people ask me, "How do you do it all?"

Going beyond mastery into a state of excellence is how I challenge myself and my clients to stand out from the crowd. Excellence is a way of being that allows us to operate our Power Threshold™ on "auto-pilot." Excellence is a standard that, when upheld, allows us to be seen by others as the "cream of the crop." But excellence can only be achieved when you have the foundation, systems, and commitment to uphold it.

You can create small examples of excellence by stating, "I am committed to always having a clean desk," "My kitchen is always stocked with fresh fruit," or "My clothes are always neatly pressed," and then making it so. Or perhaps you are ready to experience excellence in a great way, such as by stating, "I am always in integrity with my word," "My customer's satisfaction always comes first," or "Doing business with my company is easy for my clients," then making it so.

As we focused on the Power of Excellence, Sandra and I realized that it was about more than just doing – it was about who we were being. To be committed to excellence, one must make it a habit, just like brushing your teeth.

It is my coaching challenge to you to be willing to uphold a standard of excellence in your business and your life. Pick one area that if you exhibited excellence in, you could stand apart from the crowd.

One of the best ways to commit to excellence is to get someone else to hold you accountable to it. When you are willing to step fully into utilizing your power, your life will never be the same. When you are willing to have someone else hold you accountable to it, you will never be the same.

Every truly successful person I know works with a coach. Whatever you do, I invite you to identify your Power Threshold™ – know how your passion, power and profits align so you can be "in the zone." Become a master of your Power Threshold™ by leveraging your time, systems and team for a greater return on investment. Go beyond your Power Threshold™ into a state of excellence and stand out from the crowd. You can do it. Choose to be the best and you will.

Share your success story with us. We will send you a nice thank you gift for letting us know how the Power Threshold™ helped you create more freedom and wealth in your life. Go get 'em!

Randy Peyser
Publicity Writer, Book Editor, Keynote Speaker
Instigator of "Random Acts of Chutzpah"
Author of *Crappy to Happy: Small Steps to Big Happiness NOW!*

Randy Peyser practiced her initial "Random Act of Chutzpah" when she stole her first book at age three. Happily walking out of a store with one in her hand, she showed little remorse, and even claimed to have bought it herself when her parents asked her where it had come from. Ever since, she's had a love affair with the written word. So far it's been a longer lasting affair then any of her other relationships.

As a publicity writer, Randy writes power text for women entrepreneurs who want to grab media attention. She also edits books, polishes book proposals, and helps authors find agents and publishers.

She is the former Editor-In-Chief of a Bay Area magazine and a national magazine. Her interviews include: Suze Orman, Deepak Chopra, Wayne Dyer, Marianne Williamson, John Bradshaw, Caroline Myss, Neale Donald Walsch, James Redfield, and many others. Her articles have appeared in the United States, Europe, Asia, and Australia.

A dynamic speaker, Randy incorporates her signature "Comic Intervention" as she speaks on topics such as: "How I Found Happiness By Working for Embezzlers," or "Miracle Thinking: How to Create Results In Your Business, Life and Relationships."

Her first book, *Crappy to Happy: Small Steps to Big Happiness NOW!* is a best seller, and her second book, *Miracle Thinking*, aspires to follow in its footsteps.

For more information:

Inspiration Station
randy@randypeyser.com
www.randypeyser.com

Practice Random Acts Of Chutzpah

By Randy Peyser

I succeed because I do what I do, and I don't do what I don't do.I only do what I do. If I like the result, that's great. If not, that's okay. It's all an experiment anyway.

The crises in my life were multiplying faster than rabbits. I had just hit age forty, and my body no longer wanted the wear and tear of deadlines and pulling all-nighters at the Bay Area magazine where I'd worked for some years. Although I knew that this job no longer served my Highest Good and that I had to move on, beyond that I didn't know which direction to pursue. However, trusting that things would somehow work out, I left behind my collection of red pens and long time identity as a magazine Editor-in-Chief and made my exit.

Around the same time, my on-again, off-again relationship came to a grinding halt. Grieving this loss as well, I hung my heart at the door, in addition to my identity as a partner. As if this wasn't enough, one day shortly thereafter, the phone rang and the voice on the other end informed me of the suicide of a former, dearly loved employer.

What do you do when you've gone splat on the pavement of life? When the job disappears, the relationship tanks, some kind of loss occurs, or the money is stripped away? In my case, my immediate solution was to have a melt down. It was not a mere, dark night of the soul kind of melt-down, but more like a dark year-and-a-half of the soul kind of ordeal.

In the midst of so many significant losses and changes in my life, I isolated myself from engaging with other human beings and chose to spend most of my time alone in nature, walking in the mountains and talking to the Universe. I asked the big questions…Who am I? Why am I here? What direction should I take? Does my life really have a purpose?

105

It seemed like up until this point in my life, all I had come up with so far were dead ends, and at the moment, the best that I could do was to grieve the death of everything that had comprised my current identity. Fortunately, I was not afraid of my feelings. I cried the kind of tears that feel like they have no end. I would allow myself to feel the most painful feelings of grief, and somehow, I was getting stronger from the inside as I did so. I came to understand that sorrow digs the well and joy fills it. As I allowed myself to experience and express the waves of painful feelings that swelled up inside of me, I was also increasing my capacity to ultimately feel more joy.

As I allowed each wave of grief to consume me, then observed as it would disappear, I discovered that I was becoming something like a warrior woman with every passing day. Inwardly, I began to feel capable of conquering any pain or difficulty that life might ever present. Unlike most people, I wasn't afraid to feel the depths of despair, grief, or any other difficult feeling that surfaced.

As my journey of emotional healing progressed, I wanted to know if it was truly possible to find happiness in spite of the difficult outer circumstances of my crumbled life. I made a decision that for the entire next year, I would live my life as an experiment. In this experiment, I would be true to myself by constantly making choices that I thought would lead me to happiness.

If I could foresee the potential for conflict or unhappiness concerning any particular choice right from the start, I would not allow myself to say "yes" to that choice. For example, if a friend called and invited me to an event, I would first tune into my feelings and notice whether or not I felt a happy feeling when I thought about going. If I didn't feel happy about it, but my friend insisted that I go because I "should" go for whatever reason, I decided to honor my own intuition and made the choice not to go.

I also started to ask myself the question, "What's the most loving thing I can do for me right now?" Sometimes the answer would come back, "take a walk," or "cry," or "clean your desk." But often the answer came back, "do nothing." So I learned how to just sit and do nothing.

It was a time to be, to reflect, to breathe, to just sit and be present in the moment. It was not a time to be in action, in the "doing mode." One time, while I was sitting and doing nothing, it occurred to me that perhaps I could light a few candles. Grabbing a box of Chanukah candles, I sat and watched the flames from the moment the candles began to burn until over an hour later when the last wisp of waxy smoke vanished into the air.

Watching the candles became my daily meditation practice. As I would light each candle, I would assign it a quality that I desired to have in my life. Peace, calm, focus, strength, intuition... No matter how itchy or antsy I felt, I would sit and be present in the moment the entire time the candles burned. Each day, the chatter in my head began to diminish until, eventually, I could hear only the silence of the flame.

One day, from the silence, a compelling urge to sit in front of my computer and write overcame me. So I sat down at the computer and began to write. The urge began to come to me every day after that. So, every day after meditating, I'd type and watch my fingers fly as the stories flew out of me. One month and 100 pages later, I realized that I was writing a book and that this was the direction I needed to be going in.

From the moment I'd first sat down at the computer to write these stories, I'd experienced a great sense of happiness. I hadn't sat down with the intention of writing a book. I was writing only because it made me happy to do so. It occurred to me that that which was seeded in happiness could only lead to greater and greater joy as a result.

A dear mentor called me one day. As I told her about my book, she offered three pieces of advice, which I quickly found to be of great value. She said, "Randy, I want you to write out your answers to three questions: first, what is your mission? I don't mean your mission for the book, but your mission in life.

What is your purpose? Why are you here? Secondly, what do you want to accomplish for yourself by having this book published? And third, how do you want this book to benefit others?

The answer to those three questions became my guideposts for the journey toward getting my book published. Very quickly, it came to me that my mission was to "heal the hearts of the world." Since we teach most what we need to learn, guess who's heart was very much in need of healing? This certainly seemed like a worthy mission.

When I wrote about what I wanted to accomplish for myself and for others, I realized that I was writing an informal business plan. In my plan, I asked for my 'Divine Right Publisher,' and by doing so believed that whoever my publisher turned out to be would be the right publisher for my book. I wrote my ad hoc business plan like a prayer. At the top of it, I penned, "Dear God, this is what I would like to create. Will you invest?" Since I was asking God to invest in my project, how could it not happen?

Did you ever find yourself so consumed with a sense of passion that time ceases to exist and nothing else matters? I was absorbed by working on the book, spending all of my time focused on its creation.

Meanwhile my income was trickling in slower than an intravenous drip. In time, I was living off of the vegetables from my friends' gardens, and the plums on the trees in the neighborhood. I knew I had to create a better financial flow, but I didn't want to be pulled away from my writing.

One day, an amusing idea popped into my head. I couldn't imagine myself actually doing it, but this crazy idea wouldn't leave me alone. It was one of those acts that would take a whole lot of guts…nerve….actually, chutzpah! Finally, one day when the only thing left in my refrigerator was the box of baking soda, I decided to just go ahead and do it.

On a Wednesday afternoon, during the height of rush-hour traffic, I stood on a median at one of the busiest intersections off of the 101 freeway in Mill Valley, California. I wore high heels, my best dress, a new, naturally curly perm, and make-up, and held a giant cardboard sign that read, "Author Seeks Publisher."

As I performed this "random act of chutzpah," I was shaking in my shoes. After all, it was a pretty risky thing to do, and I had no idea how people would respond. The response I received, however, was overwhelmingly positive. Drivers cheered me on, smiled and waved, gave me the thumbs up sign, and shouted, "I hope you get it!" and "Good Luck!" from their cars. One woman handed me $3 as she drove by. Pretty soon, I was grinning larger than the hookah-smoking Cheshire Cat.

A publisher even stopped and gave me his card. In the end, it turned out he wasn't interested, but that was okay. I just filed his rejection slip in my "Stood Up At The Altar" file along with the others.

A funny thing did occur that day, though. You know the saying, "Be careful what you ask for, you just might get it." Notice that the sign read, "Author Seeks Publisher," not, "Author Seeks Publisher for Her Book." That evening, a publisher did call. He offered me a job as the Editor-in-Chief of his magazine. I'd applied for the position the previous week, having been dragged to the interview by a well-meaning friend. When I hadn't heard back from him, I'd thought he'd found someone else, and that was fine with me.

Even though I needed the money, I really didn't want that job. I didn't want to compromise my truth, and my truth was, my book was my unfolding dream, not another job at a magazine. Even though I was in financial hardship, politely, I performed another act of chutzpah – I turned him down. That is how willing I was to stand in my truth.

Then much to my surprise, the publisher made me another offer. He asked if I'd be willing to work the job until he found the right person. This time, I accepted. For one, I really needed the money. And secondly, it occurred to me that perhaps I could make a connection for my book by working at this magazine that I couldn't make by sitting in my living room waiting for the phone to ring. As a result of working that job, I made tons of connections that furthered my writing career, as well as covered my rent, until that company went under. (p.s… Not my fault! Not my fault!)

I continued to search for a publisher since I did not want to self-publish my book. I preferred to have the credibility of having my book accepted by an established publisher. Eventually, I found out about an annual national book show and began attending each year in the hopes of finding the publisher who would do cartwheels when she read my manuscript.

Meanwhile, I found a new national magazine and became their chief freelancer. I was very excited because the pay, which would come in the form of one big fat check six months down the road when my articles would appear in print, was going to be phenomenal.

First monkey wrench: The day I was supposed to be issued that big fat paycheck, I received a notice informing me that there had been a slight delay. Alarmed, I called the senior editor. "We're having some unexpected concerns, but we're all praying, and we're sure the angels will find a way to pay you," she said.

Thought bubble above my head: Angels? What? You mean there's no business plan?

Second monkey wrench: My sinking feeling was confirmed a few weeks later when the company was placed under investigation by the FBI. How was I supposed to know the angels they chose to pray to were the angels of embezzlement? A magazine funded by embezzled money – I had been "out-chutzpah'ed!"

On my personal Richter Scale, this was a disaster of monumental proportions. Like a dog chasing its tail, I desperately tried to reach the "Kick Me" sign on my back and rip it off. However, not being able to reach it, I instead resigned myself to slinking in misery.

To quell my pathetic wallowing, the following day I wandered into a local music store since music has always been one of the ways in which I take refuge. Offhandedly, I inquired as to whether there were any southpaw guitars. In response, I was led to the "expensive" room where I was shown a beauty of a guitar. Never an impulse buyer, the second my hands hit the strings I knew this was my guitar; I HAD to have this custom guitar.

"How much is it?" I asked.

Third monkey wrench: "$1000" came the reply.

Looking him straight in the eye, I declared, "I'm going to own this guitar within a month." Even though I didn't have the money, I knew with absolute certainty that this was my guitar, and that somehow, I would own this guitar within a month.

The next day when I mentioned the guitar to a friend, she said, "Why don't you hold a performance and ask all your friends to prepay for tickets? That way you can buy the guitar beforehand and play it at the show."

Images of a young Mickey Rooney with lots of adolescent freckles flashed through my mind… "Hey kids! Let's put on a show in the barn!" It was a great idea. There was just one problem.

Fourth monkey wrench: I dreaded performing. To get up in front of an audience and play my guitar would take more chutzpah than I could possibly ever muster up. However, I wanted this guitar so much that I found myself saying 'yes.'

The next day, another friend offered her house as a venue for my debut. So I sent an email invitation off to my circle of friends and acquaintances asking for contributions of $20 or more to support me in creating my dream guitar. Mission accomplished, I then turned my mind to the creation of the performance.

I didn't want to just play my guitar the entire time. Since it was my dream to be a published author, I decided I might as well read some stories from my manuscript as well. Over the following month, I also whipped up some comical skits to add to the mix, and a semblance of a show began to form.

First Miracle: In all, sixty-four generous people responded to my invitation, and the week prior to the show, I had $1200 in hand.

Second Miracle: When I raced down to the store to purchase my dream guitar, the clerk greeted me with some unexpected news: "We just discovered that this is a used guitar here on consignment. We'll sell it to you for $450."

Third Miracle: The huge reduction in price allowed me to purchase a microphone and stand, a guitar case, and a special effects unit, as well as pay for the church hall I'd rented when my ticket sales had outgrown my friend's house. I rushed home and proceeded to play up a storm.

Finally, the night of the big show arrived. Inwardly, I was terrified. However, being doggedly determined to see it through, I plugged the guitar into the amplifier to do a sound check. Dead silence. Quick! Fool with knobs. More silence. Try a different cord! No difference. There was a short in the electronic part of the guitar.

Now, where had this giant monkey wrench come from? First, the embezzlers and no pay for six months of work, and then all the energy I'd put into creating this special event, and now the amplification for the guitar was broken. Distraught, I dissolved into a pile of tears.

One of my friends who had arrived early listened to my lament. "Why can't things be easy?" I squeaked out through giant sobs.

"I know what you mean. Remember, my house burnt down last week," came her response.

(Darn! I was just one-upped. Even in my worst despair, there was someone in that moment who could one-up me! Couldn't I just have my own little lousy moment?)

Fourth Miracle: Even without amplification, the show was a whopping success. In fact, it was so much fun that I got beyond my fear of being on-stage and went on to create two more full-length one woman shows, which I called, "Comic Intervention for Closet Visionaries and Almost Manifesters."

The Biggest Miracle of All: One day, while I was shopping my manuscript around at that publishing convention I went to each year, I started schmoozing with a publisher and happened to mention my one-woman show.

"A show?" Her right eyebrow raised a notch. "Tell me about it." The publisher loved the idea that I was doing a show because that meant that I was highly visible in the world, and that visibility would help with book sales. In that moment, six years of frustration and disappointment as potential publishers had beckoned then disappeared ended. I procured a signed contract in two week's time and was able to begin my lifelong dream of being a published author.

The truth is, if I hadn't worked for embezzlers I never would have created a show, and if I hadn't created a show, I would probably still be looking for a publisher today. However, because of that whole experience, I wound up being able to manifest my dream, and my first book, "Crappy to Happy," became a best seller for that publisher.

Opportunities to practice random acts of chutzpah are always present. They occur every time a twinkle of inspiration to do something beyond the norm makes itself known. I must admit, there is something to be said about the willingness to take such bold or wacky risks. What I have learned is that some people will judge me, while others will appreciate me. Everyone will have their own experience. The best I can do is to just be me, regardless of the circumstances, then stay open to the magic of what might happen when I do.

Tara Marchant
Professional Life Coach, Writer, Performer and Speaker
"Mastery & Velocity Coaching: Authenticity gathers momentum"

Tara Marchant is a screenwriter, performer, Life coach and entrepreneur. She created Personal-Velocity Coaching to assist creative individuals and entrepreneurs to claim their unique voice. Her desire is that every person on the path of self-awareness live a life knowing their life purpose, and her commitment is to impact the world from a place of passion, mastery and play.

As a writer, Tara has two completed scripts and has two projects in development. She brings to coaching ten years of production, performance and leadership experience. Although Tara is known for her open and compassionate outlook, working with her is challenging and not for the faint of heart. Tara is focused, direct and committed to her clients.

Currently, Personal Velocity is developing workshops and programs using Coaching and authentic life skills to provide clarity and intention for its participants. These programs are available nationally, and in time, internationally. Tara is also co-developing a program on living courageously.

Tara holds a BA from Yale University and is a graduate of The Coaches Training Institute. She is honored and excited to participate in this "Paths to Personal Power" project and to be included in such impressive company.

For more information contact:

Personal-Velocity
www.personal-velocity.com
info@personal-velocity.com
510.500.0330 virtual assistant * 510.388.3630 direct

Embracing the Artist:
Living Courageously with your Creative Gifts

By Tara Marchant

"You have come here to find what you already have."
- Buddhist Aphorism

I love to inspire all individuals (in particular artists) to recognize that their power and gifts are expansive. Often misdirected, and waiting for external approval, the creative individual's talents and potential impact are left dormant or untapped.Where is the permission to germinate beyond convention, to be larger than the fear of failure or rejection? What does it take to galvanize behind the intention of your artistic vision to find your voice, community and a forum in multiple arenas?

Our creative, inspired spirit is our gift. My intent is to highlight this spirit that flows in all of us, which is unique and powerful. As I write, sometimes I will be expansive, which will relate to our 'beingness' in life, and other times, I will be specific, providing concrete examples of how to engage in the development of your life purpose. I recognize many are on this path, and for me, celebrating your journey with applause, collaboration, support, and assistance is my gift. So let us begin…

ARTIST MISSION: LEADERSHIP FORGOTTEN

Did Picasso consider himself a leader? If one's impact is inspirational and encourages thousands of artists to paint, think outside of the box, or pick up an abandoned paintbrush, would you consider it leadership? What defines leadership? For years my interpretation was that leadership was about podiums and auditory discourse, or wearing suits, or having manicured nails or recently shined shoes. Keeping similar imaginings on hold, I invite you to consider how your life could

116

be different, unimaginable, vast, fulfilling, simple and glorious and not at all what you find foreign from what you already know (but didn't recognize you knew, until now).

BUT FIRST...

ACT 1
WHO I WAS
THE RETURN PERPETUAL OF THE unsatisfied mind

Starring Tara Marchant,
Director Tara Marchant,
Producer Tara Marchant
Music, Editing by Tara Marchant and ...
Regular guest appearances (I'll call them my GREEK CHORUS) from family, friends and acquaintances.
Do you get the idea?

An Excerpt from the Novel

The Silence of the night fell softly on the retiring Los Angeles Street. Nothing stirred, except the occasional rustling of the leaves from the retreating Santa Anna Winds.

Staring at the undulating shadows created by the humming ceiling fan, I whispered aloud, "Am I ever going to fall asleep?" Opening the nightstand drawer, finding the bottle of Melatonin (a natural sleeping agent), I decided tonight to take a whole pill, committed to the rest I needed. Turning off the light, closing my aching eyes, I waited for its arrival and my abandonment to the depths of REM. "Please" I cried, "Please let me get some sleep."

Several years ago, nearly a decade in fact, I found myself waking up around 4:30 a.m., on a consistent basis overwhelmed by anxious, overbearing fears of failure, lack of purpose, and disconnection from my life. My nightly panics inflicted a sort of paralysis. My only relief was taking a pen to paper.

An Excerpt from the Play

> **TARA:** "Tara, you are such a loser. Does anybody see you? Sure, you're nice, smart, professional and available. Desperate! Nobody wants a desperate performer around. Face it, you're just not enough."

> **GREEK CHORUS: OPERATIC SINGING by MOM, heard from stage right:** "Oh honey, you are special. Why don't you go back to school? You could be a lawyer or a doctor. That Entertainment business is evil. Evil! EVIL!"

Do you see how unflattering these personal conversations were? They were horrifying, but I couldn't stop them. I spent hours and hours restating my inner turmoil. I knew it had to be voiced outside of my mind. Allowing some level of peace through my writing was my access and relief.

My ability to create became a liability. The ability to imagine reasons for my unhappiness, my lack of financial reward, my lack of connection was infecting my self-worth. Self-esteem, if you haven't heard, is critical to 'continued' success. I highlight 'continued' because I had experienced success at an early age. My energy, professional demeanor, 'I'll prove it' attitude, and good looks all worked time and again. What was happening? Nothing I knew was working anymore, the winning formula was faltering, disintegrating under me. This was the beginning of a process, a journey of several tormenting years (from which there are dozens of journals that "bare" witness) to a telling discovery. When that 'aha' moment came, it was humbling in its simplicity.

TARA: "How simple, it was right there, all you had to do was look silly!"

What I finally realized was that I was in action, plenty of action, but under the influence of a 12 year-old's mentality, a teenager's wants and expectations, her fears and vision. But I wasn't twelve! Heavens, it had been decades since I was that child. But I had forgotten to redesign my life while I was living it. I'll repeat that: I forgot to redesign my life while I was living it. I forgot to give myself permission to be all of what I was and much, much more. I had not checked in with my values, and when I finally did, I found out they were all skewed. Who did I want to be? Who was I becoming?

ME, MYSELF AND I: a.k.a. Isolation

Excerpt from Journal: "I can handle it," she said.

"You are so strong, you don't need anybody," he observed shyly, wondering if she wanted his company more than wanting to be alone.

"That way I can't be disappointed," she responded, looking at him directly, perhaps hinting at some unavoidable truth.

He returned the look, drawn in by her dark brown eyes, then quickly averted his stare under the discomfort of such intensity – or was it intimacy? She observed him, her disappointment confirmed. Disconnecting, she wondered if there was anybody who would ever welcome her for who she was? She feared that this scenario – unheard, unseen, fighting for connection, self worth and love – would be her life forever.

The pursuit of self is mirrored in us all. How we choose to experience it is what makes for such great drama, comedy, tragedy and musical. Do you have a favorite medium? Most of us do, and we replay our characters over and over again.

119

As an actor, my search of self was ongoing. I remember distinctly hearing my internal voices challenge me to be alone, and that my need for connection was somehow interpreted by my mind as a weakness. Wanting to love, wanting to be seen, wanting to share, wanting to be united, wanting to be included, wanting to be acknowledge by family, society, my peers was interpreted (by me) as "obviously" something I had to overcome.

Why?

It caused so much sadness and pain to want. I was convinced that the challenge was to overcome the pain I was feeling. What I could handle and win at was being solitary. Being such a good study, I became fairly proficient. The cloak I draped around me of self-sufficiency, independence, strength and needing no assistance were admirable to some but alienating to others. The cause became both a curse and a blessing.

CURSE VS. BLESSING

If I had a wish, it would be to sit in a room with the likes of Einstein, Fitzgerald (Ella and William Scott, too) or Duke Ellington, or Aristotle and ask them about their work and its evolution. I'm positive they would agree that great minds, such as those possessed by certain entrepreneurs, innovators, artists, or surgeons and professors, require a sufficient time in which one has to be alone to engage in one's learning.

The time to process an idea and the execution of its potential and impact take time. Making it happen from nothing is the obstacle. Every day is a blank slate without structure or guidance. The pleasure of your own inspiration not shackled to routine is seductive. The reality is daunting.

Does isolation become habit forming? For many it does; for me it was a shift over time. Somehow, I started as the shy, uncomfortable girl, who pushed through to the gregarious, ever-present, insecure teenager, then wound up as the professional, independent, isolated actress. The barriers to my connecting and relating to the external world grew and fortified until I was 'Rapunzel' up in the tower. Unwittingly, the status quo shifted, and I found myself disconnected from others. How had I arrived at this lonely place, far up in an unreachable fortress?

"It was Rapunzel in her loneliness trying to while away the time by letting her sweet voice ring out into the wood."

Artists seek validation through the acknowledgment and visibility of their talent, which can be observed through their music, books, movies, exhibitions or print. The time spent self-generating is "24-7". There are no paid vacations, benefits or structure. For entrepreneurs, a similar scenario might be observed through gaining clients, contracts, funding or commissions. For a scientist it may be discovering a new celestial energy field. But what I discovered for myself in my journey for acknowledgment was that I forgot to relate, and how beautiful it is to relate! How satisfying it is to have a life purpose that has impact for others, not just as a performer, but in all my dimensions and all my roles.

I am or will be an artist, writer, speaker, friend, lover, singer, audience member, activist, wife, mom, colleague, and the list goes on. Now, I rally behind those who are in search of their gift, knowing its fruition will contribute to the beauty of this planet. What I now hear, from my role as a coach, writer and speaker, are the persistent 'cries' of other's voices, silenced by fear but wanting, oh wanting something so much more.

ACCEPTING SILENCE

Silence vs. Isolation

Retreating in to solitude by choice is a gift. I admire the Dalai Lama, all Buddhist monks, and meditation disciples for the discipline of silence, and for the ability to eliminate the ego-mind as they take their vows of silence and meditation. This

121

type of lifestyle is difficult to embrace, particularly for individuals from Western philosophies. Our societal upbringing forces us towards distractions and constant material gain.

"Here in this silence we encounter our truest potential, already realized. Here in this silence. This silence, which while beyond all things, is ever present, surrounding us, hold - ing us, sustaining us, feeding us. Entering the deep forest of this silence is the greatest and most wondrous of events."
– Robert Rabbin

What I didn't know, was that I was longing for the kind of peace that comes through stillness. Isolation was disconnecting and a way of avoiding pain, rejection, longing, and desire. Silence through stillness was an embracing of all experiences – physical, emotional, and intellectual – leading to a deep knowing of self or spirit. Isolation was my attempt to negate what existed. Stillness was the accepting of what was occurring, acknowledging its existence, and then embracing it. Suddenly, the circumstances and the burden they wrought on my 'being' diminished. Now the stillness was an opening, a powerful place to begin.

"Sit quietly, doing nothing. Spring comes and the grass grows by itself."
– ZEN saying

ACT II
WHO I AM
COMMUNITY

You are what you eat. You are the company you keep. These clichés ring true. Do you have a support system that acknowledges, supports and assists you in achieving your dreams? Or does your community enable you to remain on common ground, understanding, embracing and enabling you to remain comfortable and in a status quo mode?

Let me emphasize I am in no way suggesting you disconnect from those you love and who have known you. As I've mentioned that process diminishes your relatedness. What I am encouraging you to do is to ask yourself what type of community, groups, individuals, leaders, and friends you would like to invite in. What would they be like? What would their values, their contributions, and their interests be?

Usually the answer is, "like me," or sometimes, "just the opposite of me!" If that is so, then what types of communities exist for you now? Do you attract individuals that affirm your values? If you have a value of "contribution," do you have friends who contribute, collaborate, volunteer, or share through their generosity or artistry? Or are the souls that surround you cynical or critical of others, judging what isn't there rather than celebrating what does exist? "Half-empty" or "half-full." Ask yourself, what's the cost? What's the benefit? Why are you a character in this scenario? What role and purpose is being served by your participation?

MASTER BUILDER

Inviting others in to your vision is a process often attributed to mastering success. Designing a 'team' of mutually inspired individuals, mentors, critical thinkers, and motivators will become apparent as your vision expands.

Imagine your innovative idea sprouting new opportunities just as a tree sprouts branches. Each branch, leaf, hidden crevice, and gnarly root provides something of benefit to the environment, calling forth unwittingly an entirely self-contained community. This is the goal of master building, to choose like-minded individuals who have the same passion and values, and who through their own mutual advantage, choose to rally behind your vision. Each of us is capable of creating a master building team when inspired and passionate about an idea. There is a natural magnetic force that gains momentum when a creative idea has many minds in cooperation.

During a transformative process it is critical to recognize what isn't working in the past and notice the current paradigms.

Definition: Paradigm - n.
- An example; a model; a pattern.
- The generally accepted perspective of a particular discipline at a given time.

"The biggest and most far-reaching kind of cognitive therapy is a Paradigm shift: a change in the organizing principle that underlies the way we think about ourselves and the world. It is a pattern so ingrained that we may consider it 'natural' and be unaware of its existence." – Gloria Steinem

When I recognized who I was in my ongoing drama, I decided to step off the stage for a period of reflection. During this extended intentional interlude, I embraced the adventure by dismantling the 'old' scenery, the props, and the 'stock' players, and embarked on the journey of creating new lighting, a new set, and a completely new scenario with new characters and music. That was the beginning of many new, creative inspirations that occurred when I changed paradigms.

ABSURD BUT POSSIBLE, I say...

You have a creative idea. Let's say it is a project which involves music and dance, and a non-profit dedicated to saving earthworms. Yes, there are many abstract and farfetched ideas out there. What about a crazy wonderful idea that you want to turn into a multimillion dollar company? Whatever it is, this project comes from a want that electrifies you. So you share it with your friends and family. They smile, and in a soothing voice of reassurance say, "Well, good luck. It won't be easy," or "Are you sure you want to take on something so difficult?" or "I don't know how you could possibly do that," or "But why? I thought you liked working at the company?"

124

These attitudes can dampen your spirit and, frankly, piss you off, but you wind up agreeing with how difficult it will be and you leave it at that.

Then while watching TV to numb your sense of frustration, you become engaged in The Discovery Channel, and coincidentally (synchronistic perhaps) a program on insects is on. Inspired again, you decide to go for a bike ride, to be with nature, where physical exercise in combination with the silence and awe of your surroundings reminds you of your values and sense of purpose.

You find yourself an hour later at the bike shop, getting a piece of equipment for that 30 mile bike ride you just signed up for next week. While talking to the sales person you notice he has a picture of dancing worms on his T-shirt. You mention you have a project that will save the earthworms using the artistic mediums of music and dance to engage audiences in the critical need around aerating our soil for the survival of plants.

"No kidding," he says. "I volunteer as the president of the local organic growers." Coincidentally, he plays for the symphony. This is synchronicity – the world showing up as you align yourself with your values and vision. You have simultaneously expanded your sphere of networking and have a collaborator with the same values and the same interests as you. And it all happened by doing what you do naturally and what you have done naturally all of your life. But now you have the authority to see the meaning in the coincidence.

IMAGINATION

I love art. Many claim not to have an 'artistic bone in their body.' That statement is false, impossible. To be human is to guarantee some level of creative expression. That expression may be dormant or not recognized, but it is still part of our texture. Those of us who have claimed our creative expression have done so because we have discovered that our self-expression is critical to how we relate to the world.

The creation of thought or the bending of ideas, or the

contraction and expansion of possibility or context is how the creative mind works. By choice and necessity, artists see blue as azure with hints of pink, or shadows in gray and depths of green.

Artists cannot commit to the surface of life. They explore what is hidden, what is not heard, what it looks like upside down, now with a filter of magenta, and then with their eyes shut. I love that artists can adapt and shift. They have cultivated the ability to devise a unique approach or play with options in order to ground their vision.

Web Definitions - Creativity - n

- Involves cognitive activity that results in a new way of viewing some problem or situation, and which is not necessarily restricted to practicality. (Solso)
- The ability to bring something new into existence.
- The stage in the process of problem solving in which the imagination is encouraged to soar in a search for totally new and innovative approaches.

Oh, the possibilities for us all. Would any innovator, scientist, engineer, teacher, or doctor exclude herself from the above definitions? We each have a journey in our lifetime, and applying the creative force to how we experience it is a gift. Tap into that gift, as it will be the force behind invention in designing the next chapter of your life.

ACT III
WHO I AM BECOMING
TAPPING IN

Begin to notice what in life acts as a magnet to you. We are naturally drawn to things. Looking at my life, at one point I discovered that I had a deep and profound need for access to nature. My longing for distractions from urban chaos was waning, and New York was no longer the apple of my eye. Rather, it was an obstruction to that stillness. In tapping into knowing my heart and discovering my new life purpose, I had to dismantle my life as it appeared and move across country to San Francisco. To what? I was still not clear. But I was clear that daily access to the ocean and California's large regional parks were a part of that calling. So I had to begin with an entirely new canvas.

PAINTING THE CANVAS: Broad strokes

WANTS – an exercise in stating what you want without limitation or fears around the reality of it coming true.

We all want. We desire and long for something. It can be a different quality of life, new items, better skills, more connection, or more money. All these wants are real, so why not declare them? Often our resistance from stating what we want is the fear that we may not get it. Well so what?! It doesn't stop the want. On the other hand, knowing what you want and being specific about it will assist you in your ability to notice opportunity and then create openings around your wants becoming a reality.

When I embarked from my little West Village studio in New York City to the new frontier of San Francisco my canvas of wants looked like this:

- I want to be in nature through sailing, hiking, camping and biking. Beautiful, abundant and accessible nature.
- I want to be near a large, dynamic city that emphasizes art, architecture, higher education, and beauty.
- I want to take on a whole new career path (without forsaking what I love), where I am the captain of my ship. I will also have abundant networks or crews of individuals who share and willingly take 'control' of the wheel because their course and destination parallels mine.

- I want to be rewarded financially for my gifts and my impact so that my life can include other wants.
- I want my work and personal life to include travel and learning and relating to others.

These wants are in existence now, and continue to expand. However, declaring them was crucial in my willingness to face the unknown and fly.

If you were painting this canvas, what colors would you choose for your palette? Would you want beige or coral, red or brown? For me, I knew that my palette would require brilliant, bold, surprising colors, which were necessary for movement and to draw me powerfully into action.

"Whatever you can do, or dream you can, begin it.
Boldness has genius, power, and magic in it" - Goethe.

Right now, find a piece of paper and list 25 wants in your life, from the boldest to the smallest wants and wishes. As you do so, notice if your internal voice says 'Oh, that won't happen," or "You're too old or too inexperienced," or tries to quiet down the want to subtler versions. If so, this is even more of a reason to write your wants down.

After writing down your wants without hesitation, begin collecting images, words, music, and the names of mentors or individuals you admire. This collection will be a collage or file that represents you and what you are declaring yourself to become. Are you choosing things from the mindset of 'should' or from the place of 'excitement or inspiration'? Remember, a playful life is a generating life.

"Laughter is the glorious sound of the soul waking up."
- Hafiz

THE VISION

When I first heard others say this word, I shuddered. The word was so big, so all encompassing, so finite, so abstract and so intangible. I wouldn't know where to begin. My fear of holding dreams valuable enough to declare a 'Vision Statement' paralyzed me. I had to look through the fear to understand what voice was controlling me and preventing access to the 'go' button. What was the trigger for reacting so cautiously around my master plan?

KNOWING VS. IMAGINING

Somewhere in my life history, I had made it up that I needed to be an expert in order for my thoughts and ideas to have weight and value. An expert was always something others were capable of, but something I would have to continue to strive for perpetually. This belief had been steering my life for as long as I could remember. Constantly aware of my 'shortcomings', I rarely celebrated or acknowledged my successes.

A PARABLE from the Far East
"The Cracked Pot "

A water bearer had two large pots. Each hung on an end of a pole which he carried across his neck. One of the pots had a crack in it, and while the other pot was perfect and always delivered a full portion of water at the end of the long walk from the stream to the master's house, the cracked pot arrived only half full. Daily, the bearer delivered only one and a half pots full of water to his master's house.

After two years of what the cracked pot perceived to be a bitter failure, it spoke to the water bearer.
I am ashamed of myself, and I want to apologize to you."

129

"Why?" asked the bearer. "What are you ashamed of?"

"I have delivered only half of my load because this crack in my side causes water to leak out. Because of my flaw, you have to do all of this work, and you don't get full value for your efforts," the pot said.

The water bearer felt sorry for the cracked pot, and in his compassion said, "Have you seen the beautiful flowers along the path? Did you notice that there were flowers only on your side, but not on the other pot's side? That's because I have always known about your flaw, and I took advantage of it. I planted flower seeds on your side of the path, and every day, you've watered them. I pick these beautiful flowers to decorate my master's table. Without you being just the way you are, he would not have this beauty to grace his house."

"In God's great economy, nothing goes to waste. Don't be afraid of your flaws. Acknowledge them, and you, too, can be the cause of beauty. Know that in our weakness we find our strength."
~ Author Unknown

There is a conscious knowing of what and who you are, what you know to be true, and what others see to be true in you. This is the 'knowing' of your life. What do you know? Do you know that you're funny or smart, sensitive, creative or compassionate? Do you know you're a good parent? What are your attributes and strengths? What are your shortcomings? Acknowledge what is true.

AUTHENTIC 'BEING'

To live an authentic life is to be living as fully in the now as possible, unmasking the illusions, excuses and projections one adopts in the face of uncertainty. Recognizing the patterns and owning the stewardship of their roles is critical to altering them. Who was I 'being?' I was uncertain, defensive, entitled and judging. Who did I want to be? I wanted to be inspired, compassionate, committed, powerful, humble, accessible and alive with my life purpose.

When acting from an authentic place, you expand both your outflow and your inflow of energy. In the process, your sphere of influence naturally and effortlessly opens.

Take another piece of paper and write down what you know about yourself. Consider 20-25 things that you can hold as true. This is the backdrop of what you have to build upon when you begin playing with the possibilities of your vision.

COSTUMES ARE PLAY!

If you have ever performed Shakespeare, you will know how much easier it is to perform his 'high' language when dressed in authentic period costumes. Darning the petticoats, full skirts, and wired bodices provides a reality in which the exaggerated language and dramatic prose seem effortless.

Why is this so? The costume provides a certain reality. To believe in this reality is to make it so. In time, the clothes diminish in importance as the intrinsic quality of the dancing prose becomes second nature. At this point, professional actors can play in languages designed for any time period or with any backdrop. The costume as prop becomes irrelevant, to be worn or to be discarded.

When creating a new reality for your life's purpose (like actors trying on a new language, role or costume), at first, it will be difficult and feel strange. But rehearsing the role will eventually bring you to the place of knowing what the role is, and then, you will 'own' it.

Leadership is a role to be experienced through trial and error. My personal quest is for every reader or client I work with to unearth their unique leadership gifts, and find forums, stages, or communities that benefit from these talents. Put on the costume that describes the role you imagine, write out the dialogue of the character you wish to portray, and rehearse the scene with other characters likely to exist in the scenario. In time, the role will become a facet of your personality to be used swiftly, gracefully and joyfully.

"It's time to stop being vague. If you wish to be an extraordinary person, if you wish to be wise, then you should explicitly identify the kind of person you aspire to become..." – Epictetus, Roman philosopher, 55 AD

NUTS AND BOLTS

Hoping this chapter provokes some level of insight and excitement, I will conclude with a few more exercises and suggestions around propelling your vision into reality. Reading is fundamental, however, it is not creation. Having a library on how to write a book, "does not an author make." Creation demands action, passion, commitment, synchronicity, and includes luck and planning, surrender, and of course, sleep. The following bullet points are a few essentials I swear by, and hope they become a part of your master plan.

GET A COACH, MENTOR, SUPPORT GROUP OR BUSINESS BUDDY

My greatest discovery over the last decade was learning how vital it was for me to have many voices cheering me forward. For myself, I discovered that conversations with a Coach or business buddy are critical to manifest what you want consistently. Your business buddy does not have to be in your field, but she must believe in your vision, and 'call you forth' when you get stuck and start playing small. Mentors have been down this path before you. Many are open to sharing their insights, and most definitely, their mistakes. Don't be shy, make a request. You may get a 'no', but you also might create an extraordinary alliance.

BALANCE

Balance is usually the first need to be pushed aside and forsaken. Why? Because balance involves satisfying the 'self,' which is something that Westerners have been trained to see as 'selfish' and unattractive. Since your 'self' is where your creation comes from, having a healthy self provides you with a more intrinsically powerful source of energy. For me, balance is yoga, swimming, hiking, eight hours of sleep, and socializing with friends and family. Defining my schedule to include these activities provide emotional, physical and spiritual well being. What does it look like for you? Reading, dancing, or biking and writing in a journal? Is it something that you do naturally or forsake? What type of structure could you put in place to keep you connected to a balanced life?

SMART GOALS

I use this structure constantly on my clients and myself. It may appear in different ways in different materials but for me it is clear and simple. For example, here is an arbitrary goal on one of my client's WANTS list: "I will have a personal exhibit of 20 pieces of my work in a gallery space in the Santa Monica, California area by January 2005."

S-Specific
M-Measurable
A-Accountable
R-Realistic
T-Timely

Is it specific? Yes. Is it measurable? Yes, 20 pieces will be prepared. Since 'A' is for Accountability, find somebody who will hold you accountable and ask them to keep you on target. Give them the permission to be curious about your progress and to be strict when you are distracted.

Is the goal realistic? Can she create 20 pieces in that time period? Has she ever had an exhibit? If my client had never participated in any exhibit in a gallery before, her SMART goal might have been a set-up for a crash. So if you see yourself on a potential collision course, then change the goal. Redesign it so it's doable, but stretches your comfort zone.

Timely simply requires a date, which seems pretty easy to do. Actually, this is often the hardest part for people, because a date holds you to being responsible.

SMART goals work, because they allow you to really know what you are up to and what you can achieve step by step.

REVISIT-REWRITE-RECONSIDER

Here is another tool that has given me much power and freedom. I used to be wrapped up in my 'word,' my 'integrity,' which was a paralyzing way of relating to my life. It was difficult for me to commit to anything, because I didn't want to later discover that I couldn't follow through on my commitments. I was penalizing myself and obstructing my living in the moment because I didn't want to look bad or be wrong.

To Revisit-Rewrite-Reconsider allows you to be human and to declare a goal, intention, or opinion, knowing that you may learn something in the meantime and want to rewrite a goal or revise your vision.

"The Courageous Life Program offers some great exercises to live a powerful and authentic life (**www.acourageous-life.com**)."

ACKNOWLEDGMENT

Acknowledge yourself, others and the generosity of knowledge and resources that come your way. Honor your learning, your successes, and even your mistakes. Acknowledgement keeps you conscious about your impact on others, and how others impact you, regardless of however minute their relationship is to you. Acknowledging others keeps you connected and in communication. Being connected and in communication with the world you live in has an exponential effect.

I want to acknowledge you, the reader, for your curiosity and willingness to hear about the journeys of others. This shows that you are looking for openings and I am confident, through these chapters, that you will discover many gems of experience to be useful to you on your path. Good luck. I look forward to celebrating with you on your journey.

"You have come here to find what you already have."
Buddhist Aphorism

CURTAIN
THE END

*"If your actions inspire others to dream more, learn more,
do more and become more, you are a leader."*
– John Quincy Adams

Jenny Ward
PLAY Activist & Owner of PLAYWARD

Jenny Ward is a PLAY Activist and owner of PLAYWARD, which celebrates the play-nificence of BEING ALIVE thru workshops, Playoga, books, retreats and seminars. Jenny is a play expert whose passion is to start a play revolution for people aged 35 and up.

She is the author of "*Who Said So? Creating a Life Outside The Box*" and "*PlayFul Living*" both available on Amazon.com. She teaches PLaYoga privately and runs workshops all over the United States.

Where did our playtime go? Why do we need to give up joy, spontaneity, messiness, love, passions...in order to be an "adult?" The world needs more play, and it's Jenny Ward's mission to bring it back into consciousness.

Jenny received her Masters from New York University, and is a certified Dream Coach and Yoga Practitioner. She has performed in numerous Off-Broadway shows, television shows, and films in New York City. She en-JOYS hugs, sunsets, glitter and courageous living. Jenny is the author of "Who Said So? ..creating a life outside the box" and "Playful Living." Her one woman show "Who Said So?" premieres in Los Angeles in 2005.

For more information:

Playward
P.O. Box 101
Carlsbad CA 92008
Cell: 760.521.8842
Office: 760.804.9346
Fax: 760.295.7319

jenny@playward.com
jwhosaidso@aol.com
www.playward.com

PLAY-fuLiving

By Jenny Ward

I was sitting on the beach the other day when I saw a girl with her mom digging in the sand in front of me. They were giggling as they dug their purple shovels into the dirt. The girl seemed to be about five, and was full of life and joy. There was no right way to dig and she didn't care how messy she got.

Moments later, the girl started skipping towards me. "You are pretty," she said innocently. I began to cry, not out of sadness, but because I felt loved and appreciated. In two seconds I remembered the simplicity of this PLAYGROUND called LIFE.

When do we lose this? At what age do we feel as if we need to stop telling others they are pretty? Smart? Awesome? Loved? You name it... Why do we mute ourselves into becoming adults? When we choose to PLAY in this game of life, we are choosing to be in the moment of NOW. Dig deeper into the sand and understand that the castles we build are created by the beliefs we hold.

Watching children play is watching masters at work. They get it. For years, I lived off my belief that LIFE was meant to BE HARD. I got the degrees, won the awards, got married, had the perfect home and still something was missing. Becoming an adult has many requirements: responsibility, success, marriage, stability and security. I checked each box off every day, yet found myself feeling heavy and lost. Years of dieting to be perfect, working to be successful, and auditioning to be famous led me to a great place.

NOWHERE. At the age of 28, I stopped, looked at the sandcastles I had built, and asked myself, "WHO SAID LIFE IS MEANT TO BE LIKE THIS?" From that moment on, everything changed.

I believe our world is on autopilot most of the time. In

138

order to choose your own path, one must believe in the possibility of MAGIC, PASSION, PLAY and LOVE. Play is all about believing. Believing that life is meant to be enjoyed, not survived, embraced not memorized, loved not loathed. Being a visionary takes believing in the infinite possibilities of the answer to WHAT IF? Watch a kid make a sand castle, or paint a picture and notice their willingness to create without rules, design without limitations, and build without expectations. Choosing to add playtime into your life is a key ingredient to creating a life of your own – a life designed for and by you, and magnificently lived.

I began to look at the beliefs I had about myself slowly and with compassion. "I am not enough" came thru loud and clear for me. This not enough syndrome led me further away from play, love, creativity and honor. I spent most of my life trying to please, be something I was told I had to be, and not playing within my own heart.

Life begins to shift when you decide to live for yourself. As a kid, I was taught that selfishness is wrong, that it's not "right" to think of yourself first. Being a visionary involves looking within first, getting to know your own dreams and joys, then taking steps to create that. I have re-defined being "selfish," and I triple-dog-dare-you to do the same.

Life begins on the edge of your comfort zone. It begins when you look at yourself with loving eyes and make choices that are for your highest play-full good. Giving yourself time to play, breathe, love, explore and share is essential to creating a life that is YOURS, not someone else's.

Deep down inside, we are all craving to color outside the lines, or "mess up" without labeling ourselves failures. Perfectionism bruises the soul. Play allows your heart and soul to come out and dance. When I work with clients, I encourage them to erase "SHOULD, RIGHT, RESPONSIBLE and PERFECT" from their dictionaries called our minds. These words have very powerful intentions that have been passed down from generation to generation.

"You should be this, you should do this, you better do that"… It's all over our society, leaving us with tons of ideals and expectations on our plates. One step at a time, we continue to search for the answers, buy the self-help books, take the classes, get the better job, climb up the corporate ladder and try to attain …..what? Being "successful" is a matter of whose guidelines? Why isn't it successful to take time out every day and honor yourself through PLAY?

I was tired of being told that I needed to grow up and be responsible. Instead of "going with it" I chose to step outside that box and create a new way of being responsible. Instead of struggling I wanted to celebrate. Instead of being "the best," I chose to be happy. Life became a playground, offering new slides to climb up and new jungle gyms to easefully explore. PLAY became a way of life, not something on my "to do" list. In our world I notice that most adults are waiting until they are 65 in order to play. I don't want to wait.

What is play? Remember when we were kids how important playtime was? Everyday I was outside, playing tag or building forts. I was using my mind, body and spirit every moment I could without labeling it or fitting it into my schedule. We played with all the kids on the block, not just "some" people. Race, religion, age or gender didn't really matter. What DID matter was what game to play next and how many games of kickball we could play before dinnertime. Simple pleasures. I wonder why those simple pleasures become less and less important with each birthday we have.

I believe that each year we blow out the candles we should celebrate getting younger! Dance around and declare how we will spend the next play-full year of our lives. How old are you begins to be, "Wow…how young you are!" Many people ask me how "old" I am. When I share that I am thirty, I always hear, "Wow, you look so much younger!" I FEEL younger on the inside. I believe what we FEEL on the inside radiates on the outside. A PLAY-er radiates youth, spontaneity, curiosity and blissfulness.

140

Did you ever just meet someone who has an immediate affect on you? Last week, I met a girl who was fifteen who blew me away. She giggled and hugged with her heart. I didn't have to be any particular way to hang out with her. It was simple and free, no requirements, rules, ideals or expectations. What a feeling. Her presence inspired me to be more of a play activist; to take the gift she offered by her presence and carry it with me to share with others.

It is my intention to start a play revolution, to bring back play into all of our lives, to celebrate the magnificence of being alive, to hug, share, and nurture ourselves and those around us without fear. Most of us are looking at our lives and sensing something shifting. Maybe we are noticing that we crave more quiet time, or we are watching kids and feeling the urge to just BE without the rules or requirements we have set upon ourselves.

How can we add more play into our lives? We can begin to incorporate play into our family, partnerships, workplace and personal time. Here are some play-licious ideas:

PLAY as a team with your family

Teamwork is very playful. Have play meetings where you share and create a play date. Start at home. Bring fun and creativity into your every day life. Being a "grown up" doesn't mean the fun ends. Learn from your children the purest and simplest way of being. Explore without limits and know that life is your greatest playful teacher. Create a play-full dish for dinner. Eat dinner with your fingers. Add sprinkles to the main course. Make ice cream sundaes for each other. Tell each member on your family team one thing you love about them. Create a play-full vacation without leaving your house/yard.

Partner/Spouse Playshop

What playful things can you do together? Skip down the street. Play tag. Create a new way of playing "Twister." Hug

141

every other minute. Color huge hearts together. Count the stars. Make a picnic and go somewhere new. Hold hands. Steal kisses wherever you go. Go on a play-full adventure. Wear something out of the box for you, and go out in public. Pretend its Halloween for a week. Applaud your partner for just being them! Serenade each other. Put smiley faces on everything. Write "I love you" everywhere in the house. What other ways can you and your partner/spouse be playmates?

PLAY-full Personal Ideas to Explore

1. How do you honor yourself daily?
2. Write a letter to someone you love in crayons. Send it.
3. Every day, write one thing you love about yourself (don't think and don't edit)
4. Find a picture of yourself at age five. Hang it up where you can see it everyday.
5. Start visualizing that which you have always wanted to be/experience. What are the feelings? STAY in those feelings...be in them. What other voices come up for you? Write that inner dialogue down. Notice what words you choose. Bring that sheet of paper in with all the "critics" on it. Have a ceremony to let go and recreate NEW words for you.
6. Say this every morning and every night: "I am playful and fun!"
7. Take yourself on a vacation. (At least twice a week, 10-20 minutes, outside of your normal routine). Go somewhere you have never gone before. Take a new route to a familiar destination. Get out of your comfort zone. Go to the beach and draw in the sand without making it "perfect." If you can, do cart wheels, or make angels in the sand. Let go of that voice that says, "People will be watching." By letting your soul out to play, you will INSPIRE others!

8. Begin to notice the kinds of people you surround yourself with. With love and compassion, be aware of any energy you are receiving. Does this energy feel encouraging? Make a list of the beings who encourage and support you unconditionally. Be honest with yourself.

Play with life. Life is about going with the flow, exploring and being an adventurer. Life offers many experiences in which to play. It's all on how we choose to perceive our experiences Our lives can be an adventure or we can just go through the motions, without seeing the PLAYFULLNESS life truly is about.

When you meet a stranger, talk to an old friend, walk down the street, or buy your coffee, all of this can be playful. You can smile openly at a stranger. You can tell your friends how much you appreciate them with your giggle. You can walk down the street and skip on every fourth step. You can put whipped cream on top of you grande coffee.

Life is what we want it to be. Live play-fully. Create your sand castle with the intention to be playfull, and pass it on. I triple dog dare you!

Got PLAY?

1. Roll around in the grass, and don't brush the grass off.
2. Drive/walk a different way to work, or wherever you usually go.
3. Wear glitter underneath your work clothes.
4. Wear a bright orange tie.
5. Smell a flower fully and thank it for its beauty.
6. Smile at stranger.
7. Go through the children's aisle in any store and imagine what toy you'd love to play with.
8. Buy that toy.
9. Do cartwheels.

10. Say 'yes' when you would say 'no.'
11. Say 'no' when you would say 'yes.'
12. Stand in front of the mirror and say, " I am king/queen of the universe!"
13. Call a friend and invite him or her over for play time.
14. Climb up the slide at a playground.
15. Turn the volume of your thoughts down.
16. Turn the volume of your heart up.
17. Stop. Breathe. Giggle. Look around you.
18. Remember that it's never too late to be what you always wanted to be.
19. Take yourself out for a play date.
20. Laugh at yourself as much as possible.
21. Remember you are a child of God; you are loved.
22. Put stickers on your bills.
23. Learn something new without judging if it's right or wrong.
24. Erase good or bad from the dictionary in your mind.
25. Re-define 'responsible' for yourself.
26. Selfish means "self – fishing" for love and honor of yourself.
27. Eat whipped cream right out of the can and into your mouth.
28. Hug your family, friends and yourself with playful abandon.
29. Paint rocks and line your driveway.
30. Order the Happy Meal instead of the Super Size.
31. Drink with straws.
32. Receive with a playful heart.
33. Give with a playful heart.
34. Send someone a bucket of crayons for no reason.
35. Know that you are magnificent, AS is.
36. There is nothing you have to DO.

37. Write a letter to someone who needs to play more, and tell them you want to be there!
38. Buy stickers.
39. Make a picnic and go to your bedroom for a playful intimate picnic.
40. Play with your hair, your friend's hair, your partner's hair.
41. Be a super hero for a day.
42. Stop. Jump up and down and yell.
43. Find time to laugh at yourself.
44. With your eyes, remind a stranger of how awesome they are.
45. Mow the lawn outside the lines.
46. Watch children.
47. Be messy.
48. Name each star for yourself.
49. Put marshmallows in everything you make for one day.
50. Hang poster board in your kitchen: write one thing you love about life on it in crayons everyday.
51. Invite your roommate/family/partner to write on the board in crayon, too.
52. Be aware of perfectionism, and with love, recreate a new way of looking at being 'perfect.'
53. Be confidently play-full.
54. Celebrate your body...dance naked...take sea salt showers.
55. Finger paint your 'to do' list.
56. Erase SHOULD from your dictionary.
57. Watch lady bugs.
58. Watch a football game, and blast music and dance during the commercials.
59. Order a banana split with an extra cherry.
60. Ask your children if they enjoy what they are up to - all ages apply.

61. Throw a temper tantrum if you don't get your way…(c'mon its fun.)
62. Finish this sentence: I AM…
63. Finish this sentence: "Roses are red…."
64. Make pictures with your food.
65. Eat your meal with your hands without using a napkin.
66. Pile all those you love in one bed and snuggle watching a play-full movie.

Be you. Be love. Choose Play.

Audra Baker
Personal Fitness Trainer and Coach

Audra Baker is a personal fitness trainer and the owner of a personal fitness coaching company that specializes in helping people achieve maximum health. Along with her personalized and effective personal programs, she is able to help her clients build self-confidence and self esteem. Audra is known for her ability to create a high degree of motivation among her clients to make exercise a part of their lives. Audra holds a B.S. in Kinesiology with a concentration in exercise and fitness science from San Jose State University and is pursuing advanced certifications with National Academy of Sports Medicine and American College of Sports Medicine, which is considered the "gold standard" for personal trainer certification.

"The choices you make today will shape your tomorrow in all aspects of life including fitness."
- Audra Baker

Audra Baker
audra@audrabaker.com
www.audrabaker.com
408.209.2169

A Moving Experience

By Audra Baker

As I sit down to write on this sun-soaked, beautiful California day, I'm mentally reminiscing through my life, and all I can say is, "wow." Remembering where I came from and seeing how the paths I've chosen have brought me to where I am now can only be described with the taking of a sweet breath..."wow."

How did a small-town, Texas girl end up here in sunny California, so far away from friends and family... and for what? Was I chasing some dream? Did I move here seeking fame and fortune? Did I follow a man out here in desperation for love? Or was it school? A full scholarship to Stanford would definitely warrant a huge move, but the answer to all of these questions is undoubtedly, no.

I really had no rhyme or reason to begin my adult life at the ripe age of seventeen – 2,000 some-odd miles away from all I knew. If you ask my mother, she'll tell you I was stubborn and rebellious. Perhaps I was. Though I didn't know it at the time, that gigantean decision was my first step to truly living in integrity with my deepest needs and desires.

The closest thing to rhyme or reason that I can conjure would be that I was trying to escape the realms of what I was raised to believe as 'normal.' Most of my family was middle-class to working-class, waking everyday to do the '8-to-5'thing, 'working for the man,' making a salary, and getting by month to month. I couldn't explain it back then, but I just knew that that wasn't the life for me. I've been running from that lifestyle for the last ten years – and you better believe that I am going to keep on running!

People call me brave when they first hear my story of coming out to the West coast. "Oh, I could never do that," or, "Wow, you're such a strong person", are typical comments I receive. But am I? This huge shift in my life held deep meaning and purpose,

148

but this information was hidden at a subconscious level. My philosophical decision had no cognitive connection. I just thought California would be a really cool place to live. I mean, when you only know the scorching hell and sweltering heat that can only be described as a typical August day in Dallas Texas, Northern California is like another planet. Mountains? I didn't even know what a mountain looked like until I stepped foot in this State. (I told you I was small town!).

But do you move away from your network of friends and family and familiarity for the sake of weather and mountains? Well, apparently I did. This was my first big 'adult' action, which was a precursor to many years of living in this mixed-up reality of not being able to explain why I did what I did. I just knew it was right.

What I subconsciously knew at age seventeen that I could not explain then, is now one of my grounding philosophies reflected in Nietzsche's second book, *Thus Spoke Zarathustra*. The concept of the Overman (or the Overperson as I prefer to call it) says that the key to life is to live dangerously. Pushing your own boundaries outside your comfort zone is how to determine who you are, and is appealing to no one else but yourself. (Which might explain why no one but I understood my decision).

It's the idea of taking risks in order to grow deeper into who you truly are. For me, this meant I had to move as far away from safety as I could, and make it on my own at such a vulnerable age. For many of my clients now, it is the overcoming of lethargy and emotional eating that will untie them from the unhealthy lifestyle they have become dreadfully comfortable with and accustomed to. Or perhaps, you're the woman stuck in a dead-end job living off of a miniscule salary, who is unwilling to leave the comfort zone of the same everyday routine. Whatever it may be, you have to dig deep inside to find out what it is you truly want out of your life.

The Overperson philosophy also says to strategize, prepare, and be in superb health: physically, mentally, emotionally, and spiritually. These are important steps to a fulfilling life. Gauge yourself in all four of these categories. My clients come to me for help in the physical realm, but the mental and emotional ties are what either helps or hinders their progress.

I have found that the four categories together form the cornerstone of being able to make long-lasting healthy changes in any aspect of one's life.

I have also discovered that most people do not realize just how interconnected their 'wires' really are. The most successful clients that I train—the ones that experience results – are the ones who realize that the mind/body connection is a powerful thing. There will be more about this idea later.

After making this bold and courageous move to step out of my comfort zone, I did what most would do when given an option. I found an easy path and stepped right back into my comfort-zone-land. And just as true as the laws of gravity, I eventually became lost, depressed and lethargic. Where did my dreams and desire go? Did I lose track or were they ever there?

With no need, want or desire to go to school, I found myself waiting tables late into the evening and then partying even later. Waking up at the crack of noon, making enough money to pay rent and party was the lifestyle for me. I was living in this strange reality that had no purpose—lots of fun, but no purpose. After sleepless nights with no desire to get out of bed the next day, and what some doctors described as mild depression, school seemed like the most viable option, seeing that I had nothing else better to do.

College proved to be exhausting, challenging, and way more intensive than I had ever imagined. Giving into my lazy nature, I found myself dropping classes left and right and becoming more interested (infatuated might be the better word) in men, rather than paying attention to my own life. I would fall in love and then surround my entire being around another person. I can look back now and see that it was easy to become engulfed in another, as I was never truly my own person. It's

150

easier to live through someone else; you have no accountability to your own life.

What finally got me moving in the right direction was, well, movement. Although I didn't know it at the time, exercise would be the beginning of an entire paradigm shift in my life. It led me along a path of realization that this world owed me nothing. If I wanted to live a happy and fulfilling life it would require an immense amount of hard work; carving, shaping, and creating my own paths.

You need to understand something here. I was no athlete, and even in my heightened levels of fitness today, I still have a hard time with that word. I never particularly liked sports. I remember going out for the 8th grade basketball team (don't ask... there must have been a cute boy I was trying to impress). It must have been one of those teams where they accepted anyone because, not only did I make the 'B'team, but I also warmed the bench all season. I hated running, I hated drills, and I still don't understand the player's positions.

When I tried out for track that same year, I spent the entire day of a meet nauseous and I tripped over more hurdles than I ever cleared. Can you understand where I'm coming from? I mean, for crying out loud, I was in the band! So using myself as an example of a non-sporting type, I, along with the rest of the world, still had this innate need, want, and desire to be physically active and move my body everyday.

Our bodies are meant to move! They were built for that exact purpose. If you think you do not have this innate need, it is only because you have not experienced the pure bliss and enjoyment that comes from physical activity. Your body has become numb to what it truly craves.

To be healthy in all aspects of life, physical activity is required. Through physical movement, seratonin and endorphin levels soar, creating feelings of satiety, stability, and happiness, even in times of distress. The moving body affects thoughts, feelings, emotions, and physiological processes to such a degree that it can inhibit forms of depression. Depression, which is an emotional response, decreases when you use your body in the physical realm. (Are you seeing the connections here)?

From spending time in the physical realm, you derive self-satisfaction, self-discipline, and self-affirmation; you are saying yes to life. Lethargy = lack of self-affirmation = depression = saying 'no' to life.

Okay, so maybe they are not all completely equal, but hopefully you're seeing my point. I have many friends and clients who struggle with their weight everyday, yet seem very successful in other life ventures. One of my friends is a power-ful businesswoman who is climbing a man's corporate ladder and is flourishing at the top. On the outside, she is strong and shows the world she has it all together. But I know differently. She's about fifty pounds overweight, inactive, and eats food with no conscious connection of its purpose to nourish the body.

I can tell you this same story for any overweight, inactive person. I'm not saying that people who are overweight or inac-tive are unsuccessful, but they have not discovered their true potential as a well-rounded, human being. They're missing a link. Your marriage, relationships, business, spiritual path, etc., are enhanced when movement is part of your world. The mind and body are interrelated. There is no separation.

Movement is the unity of mind, body, and spirit. Every thought your brain generates has a biophysical response. Len Zegan wrote, "For every twisted thought, there is a twisted mol-ecule." As an example, let's pretend you're driving along a busy highway. The traffic is moving along nicely when, out of nowhere, this jerk in an SUV swerves in front of you cutting you off. How angry did you just get? Are your palms sweating yet?

Let's say the same jerk does it again a few cars in front of you, and this time almost causes a huge 5 car pile up. You and the other cars around you swerve and brake simultaneously in order to miss colliding. Now you're feeling the very physical response of the sympathetic nervous system taking over, pouring adrenaline through your pounding heart and shaking body.

To use a less dramatic example, I would like to discuss the emotion of power. This emotion comes from engaging in physical activity that challenges your body farther than you ever thought possible. By successfully accomplishing physical challenges, you get a surge of physical power and energy. Cognitively, you acquire revelations of fresh ideas and heightened levels of awareness. Isn't this exciting? Fresh, creative ideas and heightened awareness is yours for the taking in all aspects of your life when you first let your body experience the fervor of exercise.

We all have it in us; it's just a matter of letting it out and finding what it is we like to do. Traditional (American) physical activities might include sports like football, basketball, volleyball, tennis or baseball. The less traditional route that I found appealing might include hiking, biking (mountain biking all the way!!) rock climbing, skiing, snowboarding or dancing. Yoga, stretching, moving meditations, *taking a walk around your neighborhood*, are all equally as great. Here's how my journey began...

I always enjoyed dancing (I never said I was good at it), so taking aerobics classes came naturally. Although I was fairly inconsistent with my regime, I enjoyed the music, energy, and feelings of well being that followed after a class. Again, I made a decision that, at the time, it just sounded like a 'cool' thing to do. Little did I know, that decision would sculpt my future.

I decided to become an exercise instructor. When I finally made the jump into teaching, it felt so natural being in front of a classroom hooting and hollering, and trying to motivate my students. What teaching did for me was give me my second lesson for success in life: consistency. As the instructor, I had to show up! Even when I was tired, sick, or feeling lazy, I was there. And the great thing about exercise is that even if you're not in the mood, when the hour of work is over and the endorphins are seeping through your blood, you suddenly can't remember why you weren't in the mood to begin with!

Have you ever indulged in one of those get-rich-quick or lose 2 pounds a day schemes? Out of curiosity, did you get rich quick? Did you actually lose those stubborn last 10 pounds in less than a week? I'm not trying to be condescending. The point I'm trying to make is that real positive results and changes happen when you consistently create your life around what is most important to you every day.

When I slowly started to see my body change into a strong powerhouse, it was exciting to see the physical changes, but the cognitive realizations were also impressive. There was a shift in my attitude. I saw that what I had accomplished not only took time, but also patience, perseverance, and yes... consistency.

Consistency has to do with creating habits in your life. What you do today greatly effects who you will be tomorrow. Let's use money as an example. If you squander your money away day after day, paying no conscious attention to saving and investing, you will have no money later in life. If on the other hand, you put a percentage of your money away every pay period—being habitually consistent—then your retirement will be looking pretty good down the road.

Creating habits that correspond to what is most important to you is the cornerstone of getting what you need most out of life. When my clients start to see results, it's because they embrace exercise as a daily habit; consistently moving their bodies toward a more balanced and fulfilled life.

When I finally realized that my own potential as an athlete and being a well-rounded person had to do with the everyday habits of moving my body, I was able to link that power into other areas of my life. I wanted something better for my life and my future. With that determination, I became the first in my family to go to college and not give up until I had a diploma in my hands.

When I made the decision to go back to school full time, my, 'the-world-owes-me-nothing' mentality came through loud and clear as I sacrificed, persevered, and over-achieved. The journey of education proved similar to my fitness journey in that the hard work and determination paid off over time. I took out student loans and stayed in on Saturday nights to study while all my friends who had already 'put in their time'went out on the town.

While pushing forward with school, I experienced a failed relationship and all the emotional hardships that accompany such a traumatic experience. About the same time that this was going on, I was taking a philosophy class that helped me define ideas I wanted to embrace as my own. One philosophy that helped me through the tough times, 'the Will to Power,' came from another of Nietzsche's teachings.

The Will to Power states that life can manifest only against obstacles. These obstacles are not only needed, but also give us empowerment when overcome. By overcoming my own emotional set backs while still pushing through school, I realized that life will go on no matter what. I will either keep pushing forward or fall flat on my face. Instead of dropping out of all my classes and falling back into my old habits, I shaped my environment by being a self-determining human being. The Will to Power gave me empowerment over my own life.

My college education morphed me into an entirely different being. Right before my very eyes, it was so amazing to see the changing and growing person I was becoming. An education has no value unless you leave the institution with more 'brain power' than you had walking into the place, and that can only happen when you are consistently focused on your habits everyday. It started in my head with a desire and it was followed through based on my daily habits.

Every amazing thing that has happened to me in my adult life has been a byproduct of creating my own happiness. I choose to be happy and healthy. Does life throw curve balls? I guarantee it. We lose loved ones, get fired, get dumped, and get cut-off on the freeway everyday. (HINT: this is where the Will to Power comes in)! But we still have the capacity to choose how we will react to every situation handed to us.

The power of choice is what has enabled me to get out of

bad relationships, finish school, and be a 'non-athlete' who races down scary paths on her mountain bike, or who carves fresh powder on her snowboard. That's what separates us humans from the rest of the animal kingdom; we can use our brainpower to choose.

The power of choice is such an amazing concept that it's almost mind-boggling. Day in and day out, minute-by-minute, we make choices for our lives. The choices you make right here, right now, completely effect who you are going to be tomorrow.

Now is the time to take the first and most fundamental step toward a fuller and richer life. Start taking care of yourself. If you're not taking care of number one, how on earth are you supposed to be there for other people? A nourishing diet and physical exercise everyday are part of a strong foundation that enhances every other aspect of your life.

Would you build your dream house on a slightly unstable foundation? The house might look great on the outside, but there's no telling when the pipes might burst on the inside. What about building your dream life? I mean, lets face it folks, you only get one shot here on earth. Treat your body (the only body you will ever have) with the respect it deserves by giving it daily exercise and wholesome foods.

As I stated earlier, using your physical body through purposeful movement positively affects all other domains in your life cognitively, emotionally, and spiritually. It's a guaranteed better way of life and you will feel more energy and vitality. I love my job and the life I have created for myself. I get to go to work everyday and help people tap into their positive energy stores through the power of exercise in order to live healthier and make more conscious choices for a gratifying life.

Using my imagination and creativity as catalysts, I realized my own path started with making a decision to say 'yes' to life. The thing is . . .of all the stories I told you about my journeys thus far (because there are still so many more to come!), there's nothing special going on here. I am an average person who started life under average circumstances. I have no traumatic past that sent me spiraling toward a destiny of greatness. I've simply chosen to live my life by my own rules.

I habitually perform my daily tasks of exercise and nourishment, knowing full well that what I do today affects the triumphs of my tomorrow. I've created a paradigm shift that has given me the capacity to realize: a) I have control over my destiny, and b) for all that I cannot control, I still can have power over my reactions. If I fail or succeed, it's my fault. If you think you can't lose weight or reach other goals in your life, then you're probably right. After all, it all starts with that ever-important organ positioned right between your ears.

Nicola Ries Taggart
Total Life Success Coach
True Insights Coaching

Nicola Ries Taggart is founder and president of True Insights Coaching, a business dedicated to helping people find their own voice and blaze their own trail. She specializes in assisting women who are ready to explore and unleash their own voice so that they can reach their full potential—personally and professionally.

Many women struggle through their days trying to keep up with the day-to-day demands of life. They feel blessed in many ways and are happy with most aspects of their life, and yet there is still something missing—a yearning and a knowing that there is a Wise Woman Within that wants to come out and fully play in the game of life. Using her experience, insight and training, Nicola helps her clients get to the heart of what matters and encourages an awakening of the voice waiting to be heard.

Nicola holds a Bachelor's degree in journalism and communications with an emphasis in public relations. She has extensive training and real-life experience in interpersonal communication, conflict resolution and mediation, organizational development, human resources and assertiveness training. Nicola is a Coaches Training Alliance Certified Coach and a Certified Dream Coach®.

Find your own voice. Blaze your own trail.

For more information:

True Insights Coaching
510.814.0891
nicola@trueinsightscoaching.com
www.trueinsightscoaching.com

Listening to the Wise Woman Within

By Nicola Ries Taggart

Too many women live the majority of their lives by someone else's definition of success. I am inspired and moved when I hear about or meet a courageous woman who, after years of following someone else's path, finally decides to start living by her own definition of success.

I feel fortunate and blessed that I have lived both 'ways' at a relatively young age – by success defined by someone else and, eventually, by me. I look back at the years of my life thus far and see the times that I listened and trusted myself, making life decisions that were in tune with who I truly was and what I truly wanted. I also see the times where I didn't—where I lived by the standards of others and settled on life decisions that were not true to myself. Neither is right or wrong. Both are my story and my journey.

I believe there is a reason why I have this story to share at this point in my life. For a long time, I have been told that I am 'wise beyond my years' and 'an old soul.' I used to downplay this, deflecting what was usually meant as a compliment, out of the fear of being seen as different or unique.

When you are a teenager, having in-depth conversations about relationships and life is not considered normal. And yet, that's where I felt comfortable, and where I was always pulled. I had friendships with women who were ten to twenty years older than me. I loved asking them questions about how they had gotten to where they were and enjoyed analyzing what was important in life to them. Although I enjoyed this, I was aware that it was "abnormal" for someone my age and didn't see it for the true gift that it was.

But I am in a different place now. I see, feel and know that one of my many gifts of is my 'Wise Woman Within.' I welcome her now with open arms. And as I accept her more and more, I hear from more women, of all different ages, who are desperate

160

to find themselves—be themselves—and shed the mask of perfectionism and comparisons that are so limiting in their lives.

I share my story with you now with the intention of encouraging you to listen to yourself. Trust yourself. Tap into the 'Wise Woman Within,' regardless of your age. Whether you are 15 or 50 or 95, you know what is right for you and have it within you to make choices that best serve you and your needs. I know from experience that there is a night and day difference in the amount of love, joy, fulfillment and passion you will feel in your life when you listen to and trust yourself, and live life by your own definition of success, not someone else's.

Living Consciously

Life can be so distracting these days, and at times overwhelming. We live in a culture where doing one task at a time is not enough anymore; we have to multi-task. We have at our disposal an increasingly dizzying array of technologies and tools to help us manage and accomplish these tasks. But don't confuse having a full life with having a fulfilled life. Although there are many positives to multi-tasking and putting technology to work for us, there are some downsides as well. The biggest one is that we are distracted from living consciously.

I know from experience that when so much is going on and we get caught up in all the "shoulds" of life, we lose sight of what is really important to us. Decisions are often made based on what we think others want or will think, or by default. If you do wake up from this unconscious state, you often do so wondering, "How did I get here?" Let me share with you how I found myself asking that very question.

When I was growing up, I was a natural leader. I was involved in things I enjoyed and expressed my opinion when I was involved in things I didn't enjoy. I made choices based on what was working for me, what I liked and what I wanted. I knew how to communicate in both positive and productive ways in order to get my point across to others. I felt my personal power in knowing that I deserved to have my opinion, and that my opinion, although perhaps not always agreed with, would be heard.

However, I started to lose that side of me after I went to college. There is not much I regret about my life. The things I do regret are not the things that I tried and didn't like or didn't do well at, but the things I never even tried at all. Much of my four years in college were years of limiting my true self. I told myself that I couldn't wait to get out of school; that the whole college experience just wasn't for me. The truth was that I wasn't allowing myself to have the type of college experience that I really wanted. I focused nearly all of my time and attention on my boyfriend (later to become my husband, then ex-husband), getting involved with friends and activities that reflected who he was, not necessarily who I was.

Although I had many memorable experiences, looking back on that time in my life, I realize that I took the easier path by not getting out there and getting involved with things and people that would help enhance my experience. I would have moments where I would break free, but found it much easier and safer to go back to what and who I knew. This was no one else's fault but my own.

Like so many college graduates, I immediately jumped into the 'real world.' I was thrilled to finally be done with school and to be considered a true adult. A month after graduating, I found a great job opportunity as a volunteer coordinator with a national nonprofit organization. I only expected to be there for three years max, as I figured anything beyond that would mean that I had become complacent in an unhappy job. But rather, I was offered new opportunity after new opportunity at the same company. I gained experience in event planning, budgeting, human resources, organizational development, patient and physician education, and fundraising; it was almost like getting my MBA on the job!

Utilizing all this new experience, I moved from an entry-level coordinator position to a manager position to ultimately a senior management position, building and leading a key department. I enjoyed the power that came from learning new things and moving up the ladder. To everyone else, my life was the definition of success. I was married to a nice man and we had nice family and friends. I had worked my way up to a top-level position in less than five years. I traveled all over the country for my job, visiting interesting places and meeting interesting people. I owned a new house in a small suburban town, and I took exciting vacations around the world.

Here's what people didn't see: despite outward appearances, I was in a marriage full of compromises that made neither of us happy. Although we had nice friends, most of them were his, not mine. I was pouring more of my time and energy into my professional life than into my personal life. I was repeatedly running late and apologizing to family and friends for not making them a priority. I was on the verge of burnout and struggling with multiple health problems. I often couldn't muster up enough energy when I wasn't working to pursue any outside interests. And when I was at work, I was struggling to keep my head above water and not drown in the details. I was living in a small town that I didn't enjoy, in a type of house I swore I'd never live in. And those exciting vacations, well, let's just say that they were someone else's dream, not mine.

So I found myself settling, depressed and burned out…all by the time I was 27!

> When you are not conscious about the direction your life is going, it is much easier to go wherever the wind blows you and to get caught up in what others think or all your "shoulds."

The simple answer to my 'early-life crisis,' (according to some people), was to just slow down and re-adjust my priorities. But deep inside I knew that there was something bigger going on. For at the heart of the matter I was keeping myself incredibly busy so that I would not have to see or feel what my life had become. It wasn't that it was a bad life. I was blessed in many ways and had many happy moments, but it wasn't my life. It wasn't how I wanted to define success.

I've always thought of myself as a pretty self-aware and self-conscious person, and my gifts do include my wisdom and insight. But during this point in my life, I was not tapping into my 'Wise Woman Within' and listening to my intuition. Oh, she would pop up every once in a while, just to see if I was ready to get back into the game, but I would manage to push her back under with concern that she didn't know what she was talking about.

So how does someone usually so self-aware, someone who instinctively lives by her heart and not just her mind, end up in this life? Looking back, it is clear that one way was by turning off all emotion. I became emotionally numb. I used to be proud of how even-keeled I was, when in fact, I was suppressing many of my true thoughts and feelings. It had become difficult for me to muster up excitement or passion for much of anything in my life at that point.

All of life's distractions had landed me right in the middle of a life that I had unconsciously created for myself. How did I get here? Somewhere along the way I had lost my true self. I wasn't thinking about what I wanted and didn't want in my life. I wasn't making decisions based on what my heart and instinct was telling me. Instead, I was allowing myself to be directed by my concern about what others would think, or even worse, by not making a decision at all. I discovered that a lack of a decision is a decision. It's just that the decision gets made for you.

Something had to change. I had to change. As I slowly started to let my true self resurface, many of my relationships changed as well. Those who liked my previous 'go with the flow' style (with a lack of opinion as to what I wanted) didn't know how to respond to the much more opinionated and vocal person I was becoming. And those who had missed the instinctive and decisive person from the past started rooting for her re-emergence.

And with this, another amazing thing started happening. I began to notice that when I was being myself, sharing my true thoughts, feelings and opinions, and openly expressing myself with others, I had more energy, excitement and passion. When I would pull back into my old ways of settling, compromising and stuffing, I felt depressed and irritable. My own behavior was reinforcing an important lesson: when I am able to be myself with people who accept, support and love me just as I am, I become an even better version of myself.

Loving Vulnerably

When you are in a place where your emotions are numb, it is very difficult to give or receive love. Opening up to feelings again can be a scary thing. Most of the time when we are living turned off from emotion it is because we are protecting ourselves from something or someone. For me, it was a matter of feeling like I couldn't live up to those around me. If I tried to be myself, I often felt dismissed and misunderstood. I had allowed myself to become conditioned to not expressing myself openly and authentically.

It took a lot for me to trust myself and others enough to put myself out there again. But I can tell you that when I did, I experienced love, support and joy like I had never imagined possible. My relationships—with my family, my friends and my new husband—have blossomed and been enriched by my willingness to be vulnerable. By opening up more to others, I have seen how they, in return, open up more to me. By putting myself out there, they too are more willing to put themselves out there.

There is power in being vulnerable, because you are choosing to expose your true self to someone else; trusting that however they react will be OK. A good friend of mine recently revealed something to me that she had been keeping to herself for some time. I actually had suspected it, but figured that she would talk to me about it when she was ready. I was surprised by how long she took to finally bring the issue to the table, but I understood. She was scared to put herself out there and be vulnerable when she wasn't sure how people would react, or in this case, how I would react. However, since she has told me and she has seen that I will love and support her in whatever makes her happy, I feel our relationship has deepened. There is a new level of closeness and openness between us since she took the chance of exposing her true self with me.

This is not the only place where I have witnessed this; in fact, I see it happen all the time with relationships. We all tend to be on guard so much these days; protecting ourselves from a variety of things. When just one of us lets down our guard to speak from our heart a small piece of our protective walls breaks down.

As I once was, many people are more focused on their professional lives than they are on their personal lives. Some people may think this is okay, and that is for each individual to decide. But most people I talk with are realizing that there is more to life than working hard and making money. They are looking for joy, love and connection. By taking a step back, consciously thinking about what we want in our relationships, and choosing to authentically love, we are able to feed our heart and soul and fill ourselves up so that we can continue to live the life we want and deserve.

> Obtaining Total Life Success is possible, but you must be willing to get out of your head and get into your heart.

Dreaming Actively

It's amazing what living consciously and loving vulnerably can do for your life. Previously, I had been focused on getting by, on surviving the life that I had unconsciously created for

166

myself. I had actually convinced myself that a life full of work with minimal play and mediocre relationships was 'good enough' and the life I was dealt to live. However, once I started to think about what I really wanted and where I wanted to go with my life, I awakened the lost dreamer within. I was able to see that my possibilities were limitless. Instead of going through the motions waiting for the next 'thing' to happen, I became full of hope, vision and excitement for the journey ahead of me.

And where am I now?

- I am in an unbelievably fulfilling and fun relationship with someone I couldn't have even dreamed up.
- I left my secure and fulltime job with the organization where I worked for more than six years to pursue my dream of 'being my own boss' by starting my coaching business.
- I have loving and authentic relationships with many of my family members and a number of close friends.
- I am full of excitement about this next stage of my life as we prepare to welcome a new baby into the family.

And I keep dreaming. For this is only one glitch on the timeline of my life. The story and the journey continue—and I am thrilled to see what unfolds.

When we actually take the time to stop, sort through the distractions and information, and listen to ourselves, we realize that we are powerful beings who know deep down what is right for each of us. I was blessed with the gift of hearing my Wise Woman Within at a young age. Some people call this God, gut instinct, intuition or Spirit. I consider it all of these things. Whatever you call it does not matter. What matters is that each of us taps into this power of 'knowing' and consciously chooses to listen and act on what we hear, even when it's not the easiest choice.

Don't get me wrong, I don't always respond to my Wise Woman Within. There continue to be times in my life when I get caught up in multi-tasking, and the "shoulds" and comparing myself to others, and I forget that if I just slow down and listen, my life would be much simpler and much more fulfilling.

TIPS FOR LISTENING TO THE WISE WOMAN WITHIN

Stop, sit down and take a deep breath. This may seem like torture to you, but you can only go in overdrive mode for so long. If you don't stop yourself, someone else will do it for you…and it may not be as pleasant. You don't have to stop for long and you don't have to 'do' anything except connect to the moment and regain your perspective.

Make appointments with yourself. This means no visitors, no phone, no TV, no radio, no anything except you and your Wise Woman. Just be and hear what you have to say. Use this time to check in with yourself and find out how you really feel about what is going (or not going) on in your life.

Remember that the past does not define your future— unless you let it. I believe that too many people become victims of their past. Instead of using past experiences as learning tools, some use them as excuses as to why they can't have the life they want today. If you believe that your past has led you to where you are now, you are right. But even more important is the fact that you have the choice as to where your life now is going to lead you in the future. You are the creator of your future experiences.

It's not about how much you achieve, it's about whether you *enjoy* what you achieve. We live in a society where more is seen as better. The more we do, the more we achieve, the more money we make, the more people admire us, the more our ego is fed, the more successful we are.

Right? Wrong! I have met more and more people who are doing lots and achieving MANY things and making lots of money and have become successful by certain standards, but they are so busy that they aren't able to enjoy *any* of it and thus feel like something is missing in their life. True joy and satisfaction comes from actually being conscious and present enough when you do achieve something that you can feel the emotion, enjoy the reaction, and relish in the admiration. You can achieve to feed the soul, or to feed the ego. One is much more satisfying than the other, I can promise you that.

Get support. Whether you form a women's group, enroll your significant other or hire a coach, having support that encourages you to listen to yourself and take action to live a life by your own definition of success can be the key to making big changes. Surround yourself with other like-minded people; individuals that will continue to feed your soul and fill your heart. Creating and living a joyful, authentic and fulfilling life is contagious. Use the power and momentum of sharing and talking with others to move your dreams forward.

There is a quite voice inside of all of us. It is a wise voice; a compassionate voice; a humble voice; a proud voice; a loving voice; and a courageous voice. Listening to that voice—the Wise Woman Within—can be difficult in today's busy and distracting world. However, embracing, listening to and following that voice may just be the most important and powerful thing that we can do for ourselves.

Eileen Piersa
Organization Development Consultant
Executive Coach
Parent Educator

Eileen started her career working with domestic violence and rape victims. She has served on community boards for mental health, domestic violence, and the YWCA. She was the chair for the YWCA Women of Achievement for several years and received the board member of the year award. She and her husband were nominated by their company's staff for the "Family Friendly Business Panel" with Senator Patty Murray in Washington State. Eileen has also taught college courses as well as parent education programs.

Eileen's mission is to help people make significant and fulfilling changes that in turn impact their teams, their work, and their families. Her clients include small businesses to large companies that utilize her skills in organization development, strategic planning, employee development, and executive coaching. Eileen has worked internally for Rockwell Hanford Operations, Westinghouse Hanford, as a Vice President of Operations for Jenny Craig, and as co-founder of her own company.

Whether it's individual coaching, parent education, or corporate consulting, Eileen's work begins with discovering individual values and core beliefs. She uses her ability to connect to the heart of the individuals and organizations she works with to inspire her clients and help them achieve their goals.

Eileen holds a BA in Family Life Education, an MS in Organization Development, and an MA. in Spiritual Psychology. Eileen brings her broad background, unique experience, and extensive education to those most interested in taking action and finding deeper meaning in all areas of their lives. As well as being parents of two teenagers, Eileen and her husband own their own consulting and marketing company, Wisdom Circles, in Carlsbad, California.

For more information:

Wisdom Circles
760.804.6271
info@WisdomCircles.com
www.WisdomCircles.com

Family: A Mirror for Business

By Eileen Piersa

Picture this: a huge boardroom with beautiful, wood-paneled walls and all the high tech gear you could dream of at one end of the room. Down the center is an immense table that stretches the length of the room. It looks like something the Giant from "Jack in the Beanstalk" would be eating his breakfast at. The perimeter of the table is lined with big, tall overstuffed black leather chairs that swivel and rock. In them, sit the chosen ones – the executive team of a major corporation. I sit in awe of the majestic size of everything and the prestige of it all. Yet it is hard for me to hold back my laughter because as I scan the room and all the faces, I see these little bodies sitting in these giant chairs and it all feels comically disproportionate to life.

This is one of my many experiences that made me realize that as adults in the work world, we are all really just big children. Or more accurately, whatever we learned (or didn't learn) in our childhood is what we bring to work with us. In over 20 years of organization development consulting and coaching, I have witnessed many behaviors in business that made me feel like I was working on the wrong end of the continuum. I often thought I could make more of an impact working with parents, and teaching them how to parent their children to develop them for their adult life and for the business world. So I decided to do both - work in business and with parents.

I have had these two paths going in my life for the last 25 years - teaching parenting classes, as well as business coaching and consulting. As time has gone on, these two paths have merged for me. I've had clients in management training comment on how the skills I taught them also worked on their kids. Participants in my parenting classes have commented on how these skills sounded like what they learned in management training. Regardless of the context in which I teach them, I realized that these are 'life skills.'

I'm convinced now that my parenting is even more important. I am shaping my children in this moment, and I am shaping them for who they will be as adults showing up to work, and having an influence on what they believe, what they value, how they treat others, and what they contribute to the world. What I teach my children will be mirrored in their adult life and in their careers.

What inspires me most is not what people have acquired in their life, or their titles or status. I am most inspired by experiencing who people are on the inside. I believe the greatest gift we can give our children is helping them to know what they believe in and the ability to know how they want to be in the world. Whether it is business consulting, coaching, or teaching parents, I've come to realize that my life work is not about human "doing," it's about human "being." The ultimate state of "being" is to live consciously in the present moment and authentically in alignment with one's values.

Our family is the first place where we learn how to "be" and how to "do." What we learn in our family is reflected in our adult life, both personally and at work. In our family we learn how to be a team; how to work together, set goals and get things done, each doing our part. Family is the place where we learn how to be thoughtful toward others, to share, to show respect, and to do what is best for the good of the whole. Our families are where we learn how to disagree, how to negotiate, how to express our feelings, and respect others' feelings and differences. We learn how to be responsible, and how to accept consequences for our choices. We also learn how to prioritize taking care of ourselves and our relationships.

How I've Embraced My Personal Power

I know I've always been an entrepreneur, a visionary, a believer that I can have what I want if I set goals and set my

174

mind to it. Partly, I was just born that way and partly I learned it in my family of seven children. I started my first business when I was about five years old, pulling my wagon around the neighborhood and collecting pop bottles. Then there was the captive audience in my mom's basement beauty shop. There was nothing like a cold glass of lemonade from my stand on the front lawn on a hot summer day before customers went into Mom's shop with no air conditioning. But I didn't stop my marketing efforts in the front yard. I made many persuasive presentations to women getting clipped and curled in this double-duty basement. I don't know if her customers really needed another pipe-cleaner-fish refrigerator magnet or a customized kitchen towel I had sewn with a handle and a snap, or if they were just taking mercy on my mother with seven kids. Whatever the reason, I was in business! Whether it was peddling trinkets in Mom's bargain basement or peddling through the neighborhood with my brothers selling crafts door-to-door, I learned a lot about partnerships, business, and getting what I wanted at a very early age.

From this experience I adopted several philosophies early in life that guided me down multiple paths. If I'd have thought about what I didn't know, I would never have owned two Diet Center franchises at the age of 24. Financing, operating, and selling a couple of franchises gave me real-life business experience I needed to get into graduate school and kick off my first corporate position at Rockwell. That part of me that is willing to take risks to try new things, learn new things, and stretch myself has enhanced my business and my personal development in countless ways.

Surround Yourself with Mentors, Friends, and Supporters

I have been fortunate to have some amazing mentors in my career and in my parenting. These people have taught me the importance of compassion. They taught me how to stand up for myself and express my ideals and my values. They have taught me how to believe in myself and embrace my gifts. My mentors, teachers, friends, and family are people, who have believed in me and in doing so, have made the biggest difference in my life. If I experience someone as an energy drain or less than supportive, I take that as a signal to beware. Over time, I've learned to let go of the people who tear me down and choose to spend time with people who build me up and support me.

Have a Vision and Go for It!

When I have a clear vision, I rarely let anything be a barrier to me. My "can do" attitude and my creative thinking, allows me to find ways to do things that others would call impossible or wouldn't even consider. I learned my resourcefulness from my beauty shop mom. I've always been able to figure out how to negotiate something or to see an issue from another angle so I can recognize multiple possibilities. I have accomplished many things simply by just holding a vision and seeing possibilities. From buying real estate to attracting awesome clients nothing gets in the way of a clear vision supported by clear intention and total commitment.

The other way I create what I envision is I affirm it in writing and say it out loud. When I started my own consulting practice years ago, I wrote down the characteristics of clients that I wanted to attract and the experience that I wanted to have in working with them. I manifested some amazing clients in a matter of months and created a full practice. Every year on my birthday I also take time to reflect on my goals from the previous year and update or establish new ones. This process helps me create the compelling vision that I am moving myself toward every day.

Your Values are Your Valuables

For as long as I can remember I have had people comment to me on how clear I am about my values. My values are my

176

core. They are my navigational device which tell me if I'm on or off course. My values help me stay true to myself and guide my decisions big and small. As leaders of organizations we model our values through our actions. As parents it is our responsibility to instill values in our kids. We're instilling values at the office and at home whether we're conscious of it or not so why not do it consciously? I have a book I call my "dream book" where I've written my mission, vision, and my values along with my goals. I review my dream book often to keep me centered in who I am. Who I am as a successful business executive, who I am as a loving wife, and who I am as a nurturing mother.

Ask for Help Before You're Stuck

There are two times to ask for help. Before you need it and when you really, really need it. Maybe you've noticed that asking your banker for money when you really, really need it doesn't work that well. There's a reason for that. The situation has usually grown more difficult for everyone involved the longer you wait to ask for help. Being raised in a big family with an alcoholic and abusive father taught me early on the skills of taking care of myself and survival. I know how to get things done by myself so it's not always easy for me to ask for help. This is one of my life-long lessons. Asking for help is not a sign of weakness but a sign of strength.

There are times when friends and family can't be objective or lack the skills to provide the appropriate help you might be asking for. That's why I believe in "professional" help; professional financial, business, mental, and spiritual help. In order to ask for help I realize there is a process I must go through. It's really quite simple but it's effective for me. First I must take the time and space to get clarity about the situation. Then I must release the Victim/Martyr part of me that keeps me focused on the past and feeling sorry for myself. And finally I must ask loudly and clearly for what I want, not what I don't want. This

177

concept alone could be a whole new book! What I can tell you as a mother, a wife, a consultant/business owner, and even as a corporate VP is that during those times when I found myself burned out, lost, depressed, sad, struggling or feeling like a failure; asking for help is what saved me from more pain or possible tragedy. It's taken some time but I now realize I don't have to wait for a crisis to ask for help. None of us creates success by ourselves and none of us gets through life's challenges by ourselves. My greatest advice for anyone struggling with pain, frustration, fear, or anxiety is to follow the three steps I have used in asking for help. Get clear about what you want, release the past, and ask loudly and clearly for exactly what you want. We must learn that it is okay to ask for help – around the house, within a marriage, with relationships, with your goals, with work, with your kids, with anything. I have learned that I am usually not upset for the reason I think and with a little help I can see what the issue is and how I can change it. Asking for help is my greatest life lesson.

Creating Your Family Mission Statement and Values

I always knew I wanted to be a mom. What I didn't know was how much I was going to love it! One of the things that was so exciting to my husband and I was being able to consciously choose the family traditions we wanted to create. We also wanted to instill values in our kids from the beginning and create the kind of home environment we wanted for our family. We knew we needed to teach by example because 90% of a child's values are formed by the age of 10.

It is important to know who you are and what you believe in. What would you take a stand for? What would you go out of your way to uphold? What are your priorities? How do you measure your success? What do you want your kids to know about how you want them to be in the world? These are great dinner table questions for any family. After numerous discussions, here are some of the values we came up with for our family:

178

- We always share what we have with others.
- We listen to each other.
- We express our anger and emotions with words.
- We are respectful and kind to everyone.
- We bring joy to someone every day.
- We say our prayers and give thanks to God every day.

We have lived these family values and reminded our kids of them on many occasions. My husband and I have also been conscious about teaching our children other values, such as responsibility, respecting authority, taking initiative, and how to be a good neighbor. My belief is that what we teach them as toddlers comes back around when they are teens. So far, that has certainly been true for our 14 and 17 year olds. I love watching them when a neighbor calls for a quick babysitting job and our kids don't charge them. They've learned when it's important to just be a good neighbor.

We taught our children the concept of being neighborly when they were little. Our neighbors to the back side were two elderly sisters. When they went into the nursing home, the kids and I had a weekly ritual of going to visit. They loved to see the kids, and the kids loved sharing their new songs and dances. When we built a wood fence in our backyard for privacy we decided to keep one section as a see-through, chain-link fence so we could keep in touch with another elderly neighbor. Our neighbor, Hildred, loved to watch our kids play and swim, and we could also keep a better eye on her and watch her garden grow with her. We also had a holiday tradition of making goodies and bringing them to all the neighbors. Aundrea and Elliot loved bundling up in the snow and walking the presents around. Now we live in California, so we are minus the snow, but none-the-less it's a tradition we continue. These actions may seem small, but they teach children values and traditions that last a lifetime.

Ideas to Help Your Family Explore and Practice Their Values

1. Write out the characteristics and values you want your child to have as an adult. Think about how you will develop and teach those to them now.

2. Take a list of values and write each on a separate 3 x 5 card. As a family, sort through them and talk about what they mean. Have each person sort them according to what they feel is most important. Talk about what those values 'look like' when you do them, i.e., our family value of "We share what we have with others" means giving our toys and clothes to neighbors or charity, giving our Halloween candy to the Mission, tithing part of our income/allowance, and finding ways to give to others that have less.

3. Look through magazines and cut out pictures of things that represent what you want to have, do, or be as a family. Talk about what the values are underneath those pictures. Make a poster of these pictures and/or write a list of family values.

4. Build a mind map of family values on posters or flip chart paper with main topics such as: traditions, education, sharing and caring, etc. Brainstorm under each topic what kinds of things you could do to these topics to make them real and achievable.

5. Have family meetings and write a family pur pose/mission statement.

6. Post your family mission and values up on the refrigerator and talk about them often.

7. Read *The Kids' Book of Questions*, or similar thought-provoking books, on car trips or vacations. Use those discussions as 'teachable moments' about values, choices, and consequences.

8. Play "What if..." and get the kids to answer how they would handle unusual situations - anything from

safety to values. For example, ask: "What would you do if you woke up in the night and smelled smoke? What would you do if you got lost in a store? What would you do if someone you were with put candy in their pocket and didn't pay for it?" The answers you hear may surprise you.

9. Keep a gratitude journal. If your children are old enough let them take turns writing down what each person says. It's also fun to do this when you have guests. You can encourage them to participate. Share "gratitudes" verbally as part of your bedtime ritual. Ask, "What are you grateful for today?"

10. Another skill-building ritual is for each person in the family to share: "What I appreciate about me is…" followed by, "What I appreciate about you is…" This teaches all of us to acknowledge ourselves, which is very healthy for self esteem. It's also great to receive acknowledgment for something we may be proud of that we want others to notice. This simple practice is also very effective for couples. Try it with your significant other for a week and see how it impacts your relationship.

11. Another ritual for teaching kids how to have control over their feelings and thoughts is to tell them to pretend there is a black hole in the floor. Anything they want to release or let go of that happened during the day can be thrown into the black hole and let go of forever! For example, a child might be upset because a teacher got angry with them. Maybe they had a fight with a friend, or something happened that they feel embarrassed or ashamed about. It all goes down the black hole. Make it silly, fun, and final.

12. Shake it off! I've also taught my kids to literally shake their bodies in order to shake off something that bothers them so they can let it go. My daughter

recently shared an experience she had while pur
chasing something in a store. Another customer
was very rude to her, which upset her. After talking
about it with me, she said, "I thought to myself, I
don't know what else has happened in this woman's
day, but I didn't do anything wrong. I just sent her
loving energy and decided to shake it off."

13. Teach forgiveness. Teach children to forgive them
selves and others. Teach them the words to say to
themselves and to others in asking for forgiveness. I
recently had the experience of coaching several
people on practicing self-forgiveness. Some of them
reported afterwards how they were sleeping better.
It's a great bedtime ritual to review your day and for
give yourself for any judgments you are holding
onto. Acknowledge yourself, forgive yourself, love
yourself, and do your best the next day. Here's an
example of self forgiveness that came in handy
when our daughter was trying out for the school tennis team and was facing some very tough competition. She kept judging herself for not being as good
as everybody else. We taught her this simple forgiveness process. We had her put her hand on her
heart and say, "I forgive myself for judging myself as
not being good enough, for the truth is, I AM good at
playing tennis and I'm okay whether I make the team
or not." By the way, Aundrea made the team.

14. Write thank-you notes as a family, and teach your
kids to write them quickly when gifts are received.
Have them write thank-you notes to give to their
teachers at the end of every year, and tell the
teacher about a special memory or something that
they learned that year. It's amazing how powerful
this can be to the recipient. Sincere and kind words
are so much more meaningful than any material gift
a teacher ever gets. My kids still do this as teens,

and I have teachers comment to me about how much they appreciate it.

15. Schedule regular "family time" and make it sacred. Nothing interferes with this time for any of us. When the kids were little, we had a Friday night ritual in the winter of opening up the hide-a-bed couch in the family room and popping popcorn while watching a favorite movie. The kids love family rituals and will do their part to protect them. Some of these rituals include coming together to end our day with nightly prayers and talk. Another is always saying "hello" and "goodbye" with a hug and a kiss. These rituals seem simple and small, but they are very meaningful and help keep us connected in our daily life.

16. Talk about and choose your family traditions, which may occur daily, around holidays, and for special occasions. Family traditions provide a sense of security and love that will stay with us always. They give us a reason to come "home." Traditions may evolve as the children grow older, but they will come to count on them and uphold them for generations to come. One of our birthday traditions is to go around the table and share one thing each person appreciates about the birthday person. This teaches the recipient to receive kindness and compliments, and it teaches others how to openly share from their heart. Make a list of family traditions you use now and include new traditions you would like to start.

Empowerment Through Affirming

One of the greatest lessons I've learned as I've watched myself parent is that the more I empower my children, the more I empower myself. My automatic reflex with my children is to sometimes judge their behavior or make them wrong. When any of us feels judged, we get defensive. When I come from a centered and loving place, and I take the time necessary in the moment to slow down, listen, and ask questions before I react, a different result is produced.

My husband has taught me much about using humor as well. It's his natural style and he is great at getting the kids to do things in a more light-hearted way. At times, his approach works well. He'll have conversations that don't get deep and heavy, but he still makes his point in a way that helps the kids to understand.

Examples of Judging vs. Affirming

Judging: (child falls and is crying)
"That didn't hurt that bad. You're exaggerating. Get up."

Affirming: "Ouch! That hurt didn't it? Let me see it. What do you think you need? Would you like some water, a band-aid, or just to sit here for a moment while I rub it until the pain is gone?"

Judging: "You drive me crazy. You are always getting into everything."

Affirming: "You are the most curious kid I know. You want to explore everything. You remind me of Curious George! Hey, why don't you go get that book and let's read it together."

Judging: "You are so lazy. You won't do anything without being told 10 times!"

Affirming: "Let's talk about a way that would work for you to get your chores done." Brainstorm ideas together. You may come up with the option for a parent to write down the chores on a check-list. The child has to check them off when completed before they can do other things. Discuss what the consequences will be if the agreement isn't followed. Then follow-up, affirm and acknowledge the good work, and of course, correct if necessary.

Judging: "Knock it off!" (What does that mean to a toddler anyway?)

Affirming: "Elliot, I see you have a lot of energy right now, don't you? The play will start in just a little bit, but you need to know that when you keep kicking the seat in front of you it doesn't feel good to the person in that seat. I want you to stop doing that and keep your feet still, please. Thank you. Hey, sing me that song you learned today."

Judging: "What do you mean you want the car again? You've hardly been home this week!"

Affirming: "You are having a great summer. I hear that you want to go out with your friends again and I know how important they are to you. So let's sit down and look at your proposed schedule for the next few days and compare it to my schedule. Let's talk about my expectations for the next few days so we can work out a plan that works for both of us."

What did you notice between the options of judging and affirming? How would you feel being the recipient of judgments or affirmations? What is the difference in the impact to someone's self-esteem between these two approaches? Which one motivates you or your child more? How much time does it take a parent to get his/her way with a judging tone as compared to a positive and affirmative approach? My experience is that my quick judgment approach might feel more efficient at the time, but the results don't last as long. How do we judge or affirm in the workplace? How well does that work?

When I respond in an affirming way and involve my child in a "teachable moment," it takes more time, but the results are better. When I listen and validate my children's feelings, I enhance their self-esteem, and encourage problem-solving skills and support their creativity. An affirmative approach models how to take time to have a loving relationship; how to talk, how to listen, how to resolve a conflict, and how to treat a friend. Wouldn't this be great for all relationships? Relationships take time, effort, energy, thought and love. That is how we all thrive. As I've continued to learn this over and over in all areas of my life – as a spouse, parent, employer, co-worker, friend, daughter, sister, neighbor – it all comes down to one thing — life skills.

Words Become Labels That Stick for a Very Long Time

Which would you rather hear: "You are so curious!" or "You are into everything and you drive me crazy!?" I remember when my son was going through the "power and identity" stage, which is common among 3-6 year olds. He was constantly testing out his personal power. I would often talk to him about how powerful he was or how curious he was. Then he would say, "Mom, I am really curious aren't I? I love to learn about new things." He would also tell me, "I am so powerful." Rather than fight his learning process, I learned to embrace it and enjoy it. I can tell you that he is both curious and powerful, even today.

A wonderful lesson I learned from a friend with three gorgeous daughters was that it's not so much what I say to my daughter that she will hear, it's more about what I say to myself. She warned me to not criticize my body in front of my daughter, or my teen might embrace that message, instead of absorbing all of the wonderful things I say to her. I'm so grateful she gave me that advice early on. We learn by imitation and repetition, and children take on our self-images, too.

Be careful how you label your kids, yourself, your friends, or your family. Words become labels and they often stick for a very long time. They create your reality and your children's reality. Remember, everything you say to your child tells them who they

186

are and how important they are to you, as well as how important we are to ourselves. So choose positive words.

Guide Them to the Next Stage of Development

I had a CEO ask me recently if we couldn't just expect everyone to be efficient in their communication and not have to take so much time to discuss things. I agreed with him that people could become more efficient in their communication and meeting skills, but everyone's communication skills are at a different level of experience and ability. What about a new employee who needs training for their position? How does a parent with no training or experience suddenly have the ability to teach her children to be "efficient" in their communications? It's just not realistic. We have to look at what is developmentally appropriate for our staff, our children or any relationship. Training and development take time and consistency to bring a family or company to a higher level of communication skills. Compassion and patience are essential when growing children and employees.

Sometimes I have to stop and remind myself that my kids are ready to progress to the next stage and take on more responsibilities. We'll have a conversation about how well they are doing with the many things they're responsible for, and how it's now time to take the next step in their development and expand their responsibilities. For example, "Elliot, you are now tall enough and strong enough to use the lawn mower." The same is true for employees. It is truly wonderful to have parents, employers, and loving partners in our lives that support us in continuing to learn and grow, as we are never done developing our life skills.

Teach Them to Think for Themselves

One of the most important things we can give our kids is the gift of thinking for themselves. Instead of telling them what their options are, ask them to tell you. Get them to think forward. Once you get a sense of what your child is thinking, you can guide her along with other ideas, which will ultimately get her to think even deeper. I started this process early on with my kids by using fairy tales as an example. I would ask, "What other choices did Cinderella have?" or "What else could Hansel and Gretel have done to get away from the witch?" When you teach them to ask more questions you teach them to think for themselves.

Another example happened when we were having one of those rough mornings when everyone was harried. We were getting in the car to go to school. I buckled everyone in (including my daughter's two imaginary friends), then ran back in the house for a forgotten item. My reflex was to yell at the kids for not being more cooperative and moving faster. I expected them to instantly respond to my short, terse commands but it didn't work that way.

Rather than repeat this scene every day and try to get their response by yelling louder or starting earlier, I found the think-for-yourself approach much more effective. I would encourage deeper thinking by asking open-ended questions, such as, "When we have a morning that goes really well with no rushing or yelling, what do we do that makes that work?"

We would brainstorm solutions, such as putting out our clothes and packing lunches the night before. We also found that if the children told us how they wanted to be awakened, they were more cooperative in getting out of bed. For instance, our son likes to have his back rubbed while we talk to him for a few minutes. The waking transition is much more pleasant for everyone this way. Once you change your focus from problem solving to focusing on what you want, your children will see the benefit of starting to think for themselves.

This is also a great skill to learn in business. A manager can guide her team to think about and focus on questions, such as, "When we are working at our best, what does it look like"? Or "When we've completed a project on time and on budget, what has contributed to that success? How do we do that again, even better?"

Give Them the Gift of Faith

One of the greatest gifts my mom gave me was my faith. Her "Let go and let God" mantra from Al Anon has been a part of me forever. It's a gift I'm passing on to my kids. Prayer has always been a part of our family's bedtime ritual, even now with teenagers. I believe that asking for Spirit's assistance, remembering others who have greater needs than us, and expressing gratitude for all that we have, are very important to keep a healthy perspective on our daily lives.

When my children were in grade school, we kept a written gratitude journal as a family. As I mentioned in Step 9 above, the kids loved it when we had company and we would invite our guests to participate in our family journal writing. Now we share our gratitudes and appreciations verbally along with our bedtime prayers. Our children have evolved over the years from "I'm grateful for my dog and my toys" to sincere gratitude for our family, for someone's help, and for teachers and friends. Our family's faith and appreciation of the blessings we have seems to get stronger as our gratitude list gets longer.

Allow Them to Feel Their Feelings

From the time my kids were toddlers, I taught them about their emotions. We talked openly about joy, anger, frustration, sadness, excitement, and disappointment. I knew our children would be better communicators and better mates, employees, and leaders if they understood that life is not perfect and that we don't always get our way.

Our children know that it is perfectly fine to express their emotions with words, laughter and tears. They know that life includes a wide range of ups and downs. They are much more empowered to face anything life throws at them when they are able to acknowledge their emotions and make a conscious choice of how to respond.

When my husband and I have disagreements and one of us is upset, we don't shelter our children from seeing our emotions. We aren't abusive or talk about topics that are not appropriate for our children, but as parents, we both agreed it was important for our children to see that there is nothing wrong with expressing an emotion as long is it is done with words and respect. Our children always know that we will work through our disagreements, no matter how challenging.

Doing My Best Every Day

How do I be the best parent, spouse, co-worker, or boss I can be? I do my best every day. I gave up the image of being super-mom a long time ago. It amazes me how people assume that I have it all together, and that I am always in control, balanced, and able to handle everything perfectly. I don't even strive for that anymore. I realize that I am being my best when I am taking care of myself first. When my cup is full I can give so much more to others, especially my family.

When I am being my best I come from a place of peace and calm. There are so many things that happen in a day that give us the opportunity to choose our emotions and responses. One of the things that helps me is something I taught the kids when they were little. When milk would spill or something would break I would say, "Oh well. These things happen. We can always get some more milk, but we can't get a new Elliot or Aundrea or a new mom or dad." I wanted my children to keep a perspective on life and not put "things" above people. As long as we are okay, then nothing else matters.

Over the years, the kids have learned to mirror this little saying back at just the right moment. One time, our expensive, one-week old, green and burgundy couch mysteriously displayed a big, white bleach stain on a cushion. My husband had used Elliot's plastic baseball bat to stir some pool chemicals and some of it had dripped into the tiny hole on the end of the bat. Elliot then brought it into the house and dropped it on the couch. Once we solved the mystery the kids said to us, "Oh well. These things happen. We can always get a new couch, but we can't get a new Elliot!"

My husband, who was so upset with himself, had to laugh and let it go. We were also grateful that this chemical didn't hurt anyone. So we flipped over the cushion, and all of us and the couch have been fine for the past 10 years.

Although I wouldn't exactly say, "Oh well. These things happen" at work, I know that the responses we have in business settings are formed by the attitudes we developed in our earlier years. Can you imagine a work place where our communications were based on these same principals and values? Principals and values based on acceptance, love and empowerment?

When I am in judgment, I create a very unpleasant reality for myself. However, when I am doing my best, I am taking care of me, choosing peace and calm, and acting from a loving place. When I come from a loving place, I see things differently, I hear things differently, and I respond differently. When I use a loving approach, I am forgiving of myself and others. I am fully present, am learning from my past, and am able to face anything that the world hands to me. I empower myself when I brush past the "surface stuff" and live from the depths of my authentic self with peace, love and grace.

Teach Skills for a Lifetime

Regardless of how any of us chooses to see the challenges of parenting, running a business, or just getting through life, most of us will agree that becoming a better parent, partner, employee, or leader will make this world a better place. Our abilities to understand and guide our children as they grow up and take over a more complex and challenging world are more important now than ever before. The skills and tools we

191

provide our children today will be mirrored in the boardrooms of the companies that drive our world tomorrow. There are certainly plenty of ways to overindulge our children, but we can never overdo respect, nurturing and love.

The blending of parenting skills and business skills creates the life skills that are important for every relationship:

- Being fully present by showing up physically, mentally, emotionally, and spiritually
- Actively listening – removing all distractions and focusing on the other person
- Knowing what I believe in and what is important to me
- Seeing the other person in a loving and affirming way
- Choosing my words carefully to empower myself and others
- Consciously modeling behaviors that others learn from
- Encouraging others to express their feelings in healthy ways
- Guiding others toward continuous personal development

There is little difference between the skills we teach a child and the skills we teach our workforce. As we look in the mirror, we see the reflection of all that we've experienced, learned, and practiced. The skills given to our children, either through conscious effort or simply by modeling our behavior, become the foundation for our workplace, our community and our world.

Michelle Randall
Executive and Political Leadership Coach
Principle of The Juncture Company

Michelle leads the Juncture Company from her lakefront home in the oak studded hills of California, just 30 minutes from the heart of Silicon Valley. From this inspiring location she is a powerful ally for leaders in business and government around the world, as they take their organizations to ever-greater heights while personally achieving aligned, thriving lives with courage and grace.

Michelle understands the complex world of her clients. As an executive in the construction and high tech industries she successfully guided CEOs into profitable new markets and industry victories. Values-based leadership is fundamental to Michelle. She aided in the transformation of home building, by delivering the first green building materials product line in the nation and educating builders throughout California and the US green building practices. She ran marketing for a start up company seeing it through launch with analysts and the media to bringing the products to market. She embedded cutting-edge environmental values in an 80-year-old lumber company with umbrella responsibilities for marketing, finance and operational activities having impressive financial results. Michelle continues her involvement in the sustainability field by providing workshops addressing the unique leadership issues for socially responsible organizations; as an advisor to the Sustainability Academy; and by directing member education for the Investors' Circle, the only nationwide sustainability-based venture capital network.

Michelle's experience spans the globe. During college she represented the University of California in the Soviet Union as part of a cold war cultural exchange, meeting with party emissaries during the day and in the evenings sharing black market vodka with young leaders of change in the evenings. She lived in Germany for years, part of that time working at Deutsche Telecom, the world's third largest telecommunications company, where she hosted senior level delegations from Africa, Asia and the Middle East while working for the CEO. Michelle earned a Masters of Business Administration from the Fisher School of International Business, is a graduate of the Coaches Training Institute, a Certified Professional Co-Active Coach, and a member of the International Coach Federation.

In addition to executive coaching, Michelle gives talks and workshops for professional women to invite them on a journey of transformation to live their bold legacy. For a schedule of her upcoming events or to request her as a speaker, please visit her website.

The Juncture Company
Everyday is a juncture – choose your legacy.
visionarywomen@juncturecompany.com
www.juncturecompany.com

Living a Bold Legacy: A Toddler's Paradise

by Michelle Randall

Legacy. It's a big-sounding word that conjures up images of important people and momentous actions. The implications can make a person feel big and small simultaneously. "I can have a legacy, but what would it be? I'm not JFK or Nelson Mandela. I'm just me." If you look it up, the word legacy simply describes a gift; how we will be remembered. In this moment, you are already living your legacy and so am I. The question is not whether or not we will leave a legacy, since we will do just that by being here and living our lives; the question is, are we creating the legacy we want?

The future will remember us kindly for the contributions we made to other people, and the community as a whole, as long as we have lived our lives in integrity. Not surprisingly, making a significant contribution to other people and the community as a whole, and living out our values in a healthy way, are also the keys to living a fulfilling life. This means that the best part of creating the legacy we want before we die is that we get to live it. It's like giving a gift to the future and being at the party to watch the delight on the recipient's face as it is unwrapped.

When I graduated from business school I wanted my legacy to be about creating a more sustainable relationship between business and the environment, and I was itching to make a significant impact on the world. I was thrilled to find great and meaningful work as a change agent within an eighty-year-old lumber company. The young, innovative CEO wanted to see if a financially successful, environmental product line could be developed, and I wanted to prove to the entire industry that it could be done. What was to become clear to me was that I was chillingly alone in this desire. Every expert I spoke with assured me in no uncertain terms that I was on a fool's mission. I had willingly wandered into a deeply entrenched industry that could agree on one thing: 'tree huggers were the enemy.' And I stood there – young, female, 'green' in many ways, overeducated, not from the industry, and determined to succeed or die trying. While I would ultimately become very successful in achieving my goals, I would practically achieve both by courting the collateral damage of self-destruction and self-neglect.

Ambition, drive and the desire to take on enormous challenges are well respected attributes. What gets a bit murky is when these attributes can drift into masochism. This shadow side is often what stops many people from even dreaming of creating their bold legacy, mainly because there is an assumed association between legacy and tremendous suffering. They'll ask, 'Would Nelson Mandela's legacy be what it is without the decades he spent in jail?' Maybe not, and while that is part of his story, that is not the whole story. His legacy may be a bit more legendary as a result of his suffering, however his legacy is of leadership, vision, integrity and steadfast courage. These are at the core of a powerful legacy; suffering does not need to be.

What gets confusing for many people is a belief that the amount of suffering that goes into surmounting a huge challenge determines the importance of the person undertaking it. I know I had this confusion by believing that in order to achieve success I had to suffer, and that my suffering would somehow make my contribution and me more important. I now know that it was taking action on behalf of my beliefs and values that was noble and important. The suffering actually detracted from any success I achieved because it pointed to a lack of power created by not valuing myself intrinsically.

Today I choose to be bold and take action about what I believe in, but not because I think it makes me more important; it's just me naturally living my values out loud and in a way that nourishes my whole self. So do I believe you have to make huge sacrifices to live a legacy you are proud of? Hell no! Look around. There are plenty of examples of people powerfully living their legacies without suffering, and I'm one of them.

But I'm getting ahead of myself. The ways that my beliefs about suffering slung my life out of alignment were numerous. Here's a view into the thorny road I was speeding along… Back at the lumber company, I was working to prove the naysayers wrong by falling over myself to provide outstanding service to anyone in the company who was willing to work with me, and any builders whose interest I could capture. To make this happen, I spent a lot of time at people's beck and call, driving about 60,000 miles a year up and down California's Central Coast. I was working 10 to 12 hours each day, and I was away at events talking about environmental building materials most weekends during the summer. Over time I packed on about 40 pounds, was rarely at home with my husband, and racked up a number of speeding tickets.

Since we're talking about one's legacy, it's important to note that I wasn't careening along in tenuous control of my life because I wasn't living my values. Instead, it was because of how I was living them. What had me so out of alignment was that while I knew that my noble values of contribution and achievement were important, their evil twin – the value of suffering – let them get so big and overwhelming that they had eclipsed my other values around family and friends and rendered my health and sense of life balance a complete farce. Because values are the concepts that are core to who we are and how we act in the world, when they run amok and unchecked they can act like bullies, beating up our other values and pushing them into the corners of our lives. It is when we are conscious of all of our values and how we want to live them out in alignment with each other that we can step in and recognize the brutes within us.

Until I did that, this case of values beating up other values had me furiously spinning like a top and wobbling from lack of alignment. But at this point, things were far from being totally out of control. In fact, my suffering from lack of alignment seemed to help earn the success I started to enjoy when my efforts began proving the experts wrong. My environmental product line turned into quite a financial success, generating $1 million in revenue in its first year. It opened up new cities for the company and attracted new builders to us. My efforts started to get us national recognition and some of the builders in our area started to meet and lobby to change construction practices. Some former naysayers within the company became allies and even advocates. I was invited to speak at national and international conferences and numerous articles were written about my work.

When I was promoted to an executive in the company I started to feel that I had arrived at my success. I had mastered a monumental challenge, but somehow I didn't really feel successful. It was like if I could achieve it, then maybe the arena I was playing in wasn't big enough. So true to form, I started looking around for a bigger, 'badder' challenge to go after.

At that time, the high-tech boom was in full swing and it seemed larger than life, at the cutting edge of business practices, and the whole world was talking about it. It was the biggest arena around, so I wanted in, and there was no welcome mat.

'Great achievements, wrong industry,' was the rejection I received, and the more I was pushed away the more I was determined to get in the door. By the time I broke into the high-tech arena, my value to achieve was on hyper-drive, and at this point had drowned out its sister value of contribution. So I left my business and environmental work behind in order to market a high-tech doo-dad.

I had to work to convince myself that I was, indeed, on a new path of making a contribution; it would just be indirect this time. I was going to be a pivotal part of launching a minority-owned company, and I was as swept away as any by the hype that we were going to be hugely successful and all become millionaires. I told myself that if this was going to be the case, instead of being the change I wanted to see in the world, I could buy the change instead.

I was hardly alone. There were plenty of us thinking that we

198

could purchase our way to a legacy of contribution, and despite the burst bubble, this is still a popular notion. I call this way of thinking 'Ghandi-gone-Gucci.' For me, it turned out that compromising my way of thinking about my legacy in this way would become my personal unraveling point.

I certainly didn't notice this right away, wrapped up in the heady environment of a start-up company. We shared the beliefs common among start-ups that we were forging new ground; that we had figured out something that everybody else had missed for the moment; and if we were speedy and stealthy we could achieve that big launch and wealth and freedom would follow.

It didn't take long before I was promoted from managing our core product to running the marketing for the entire company. This meant I was flying across the country several times a month to high-level meetings with partners and analysts, newspapers and magazines. I felt heady with importance - I was a high-tech executive and it was a wild ride.

As part of the ride, I was now working more that I ever had before and with complete focus – I was in an all-out sprint. I was no longer commuting two hours a day. Still, I was leaving the house earlier and returning later. Every Saturday morning started with a senior staff meeting that grew to consume most of the day. Weekend getaways were impossible, and when I took a week's vacation it was practically considered treason. I felt out of control like you feel when you run too fast and struggle to stay on top of your own feet. I recognized this and started working just 50 hours per week. This left me feeling completely behind and even more stressed out, so I quickly abandoned it.

As you know, the reason it is very dangerous to drive a car that is out of alignment at high speeds is that it is always pulling to one side. So, as the driver you are always making an effort to steer just in order to go straight. Then, if something unexpected comes into your path, any compensation on your part is magnified and the system quickly tumbles out of control. And you can crash. Big time.

Of course, a life out of alignment is equally disastrous to drive at high speeds for all of the same reasons. The alignment in my life had been degenerating more and more over time, and I was pulling with all my might just to make headway.

When I got the call that my brother died, it was more than a bump in the road. I was devastated and my grief was so overwhelming that all I wanted to do was hole up by myself and bleed in private. And the rest of the world marched on. I took a few days off, isolated myself in my cubicle, and managed not to travel for a few weeks.

In order to regain my sense of living, I finally heeded my husband's urgings to have a child after five years of marriage. While conditions weren't ideal, we figured they never would be and trusted we'd figure it out. In my work I saw my only surviving legacy – namely achievement – threatened. I had not been at the top of my game while reeling from my brother's death, and if I didn't get back into gear I believed I'd soon find myself retired to the mommy track and among the huge ranks of underemployed, previously-professional women who were unable to get back into the workforce. Playing not to lose, I steered back into the fast lane.

By this point, I certainly had inklings, but hadn't gotten the full message of how radically I needed to redesign my life. I kept thinking I could make things work with small adjustments and compensations. So either my lack of control left me a magnet for disaster or the messenger got more determined to get my attention. Within a period of two weeks, my grandma was diagnosed with cancer, our car was stolen, my company threatened to close it's doors, my husband briefly lost his job, and the life that had breathed within me went out. As a result of the miscarriage, I grappled with secondary infections and left work on disability.

I was then faced with plenty of time to evaluate a life I had lost so much control over that at a young age I couldn't even ironically say that, 'at least I had my health.' The universe had my attention, and ready or not, I was listening.

200

Now, my story would fit a great dramatic curve if as soon as I got the message that it was time to radically change my life that I actually did it. I would so love to be able to say that I got the message, made the sweeping changes, and it was smooth sailing from then on. For certain, I got the message that it was time to change. It seemed clear that I had probably been lucky to have a miscarriage because I needed to figure out the way I wanted to live my life before bringing someone new into it.

I acted on the message in a measured and rational way, by quitting my job at the start-up once I had a great job offer in hand. But the trick was that the foundation that had been driving my behavior didn't just shift once the light bulb went off. Instead, it was going to take a lot more learning and rigor to make more of the hard choices that led me to change. I had been running with all my might for a long time and what I really needed to do was learn how to walk.

As I watched my daughter learning to walk, her unselfconscious determination amazed me. Her precious head was covered with goose eggs and she was bruised from all the tumbles she was taking. Still, she kept going without a thought about giving up. One evening, I sat and watched her spend half an hour in which she fell twenty times in order to move forward less than two feet. She considered quitting just as little as she considered the momentousness of what she was learning to do.

In the moment, I shook my head thinking that as adults we would never learn to walk; that after landing on our cans a few times we'd declare that we just weren't cut out to be walkers. We'd tell ourselves that we were meant to be doing something different, otherwise it wouldn't hurt so much. We'd point to some personality test we'd taken that proved that we just didn't fit the walking profile. And while parts of this might be true, the reality is that my story is really about learning to walk.

Once I started shifting the focus of my life from career to being a complete person I was taking lurching steps and learning about balance. I fell plenty of times and it hurt. Still I kept getting up and gathering the courage to find myself on my feet again. And if I can do that, then anyone can achieve a thriving and complete life. My first step was to find my footing.

The job offer I had when I left the start-up fit all my old criteria for success. It was a big name company and the job was challenging, I could be evolving an entrenched industry toward environmental sustainability, and it even had the desired but never realized downtown location, the top-floor office, and even the click of high-heels along a granite floor in the foyer. What also came with it were grueling work hours, a punishingly competitive office environment, and, well, you get the picture.

So did my husband and I. He thought it would be a terrible decision to take the job. I assured him that this time it would be different, that this time, I would have to work the unbelievable hours just until I was established during the first year or two. Afterward, I would be guaranteed total flexibility with my time as long as the results kept perpetuating themselves. My husband was more difficult to delude than I had been, but then again the expectations I had for myself and my need to prove I was successful were still running the show.

This would be a great time for a revelatory moment when I came to my senses, refused the offer with a confident smile on my face and strode off into the sunset. I know it would be great to write. Instead I took the offer.

And I was saved by the bell. It rang in the form of a clause buried in an employment contract that was faxed to me a few days before I was set to start work. I couldn't live with the clause and my prospective employer wouldn't budge on it. For me, it would have been a deal with the devil.

I sat there with the decision for my life in front of me in black and white. I could sign the contract and commit to my old ways, or leave it on the table and commit to living my life in a way that I didn't yet know how to do. I felt like I would be stepping into nothing – a completely unknown way of being. Finally, I can say I made the bold and courageous choice, and while I wasn't striding, I turned and walked away.

I ended up spending a lot of time walking that summer. I

was training to participate in a three-day money-raising event of walking sixty miles from San Jose to San Francisco to benefit breast cancer research and treatment. Since I now wasn't working or even looking for work, I spent weeks experiencing the place I called home in an entirely new way.

Walking along roadways that I usually drove, I started to witness all of the aliveness I was a part of. Now that I wasn't running at breakneck speed, I saw squirrels and deer, snakes and rabbits, in unexpected places for the first time. I even encountered a mountain lion one afternoon.

In the aliveness, my own awareness had a chance to stretch out of the narrow band I had confined it to. I was filled with wonder and delight in my experiences. However inside of me, I also felt profoundly sad and embarrassed, wrestling with a deep belief that I had failed. Then I found the keys to the footlocker in my mind that I had stuffed my intuition into, and afraid as I had been of having it be labeled "women's intuition" in men's industries, I let it free. Magic started to appear.

Losing my salary had been a major financial blow. While we hadn't been living lavishly, we were living in the San Francisco Bay Area and had been doing a fairly good job of ignoring our finances. The whole time that we had been earning loads of money, we always felt broke. When I left my job and refused the job offer, we weren't sure if we would be able to keep making our mortgage payments.

Now that we weren't always in a rush, I began to devote more attention to our finances and our spending patterns. We had more time so we stopped eating out constantly and making spontaneous purchases. Instead, we slowed our thinking and made better financial decisions. One of the best things we did was to ban the words, 'we can't afford it' from our vocabulary. Instead, we focused on what 'we chose to afford.' As a result, we kept our house, and started living much more comfortably than we had been previously. The wind was at our backs, so I kept walking.

It is an amazing experience to spend hours each day alone,

your feet in contact with the earth. The rhythm is mesmerizing and it frees the mind for exploration. I dug into my sense of failure to ask what success really meant to me. In doing so, I realized that my definition of success was frozen from when I was 16 years old. It was long overdue for my relationship with "success" to evolve, and evolve it did.

In some ways, it seems funny today that I even grappled so significantly with the whole notion, because from where I sit, the whole concept of success seems insignificant. I know that achievement makes for good marketing, but fulfillment has another source altogether. I've also learned that success is not a destination, rather, it is one way of looking at an outcome. The only way to really not succeed is to get an outcome I'm not happy with and to fail to learn anything from it or quit.

The 3-day event I had been training for spanned a distance that could have been driven in one hour. When the organizers had said it would be a life-changing experience, I thought they were overdoing it. As it turns out it was a true life-awakening event. I got to spend three days with 4500 other people who shared my huge value for contribution, and together we made up a mobile monument to passion, survival, and defiance.

I saw shadows of my old way of being when the values of achievement and contribution got out of control in others, in First-Aid tents so dehydrated they laid on cots hooked up to IV's, or as they moved forward on crutches. It filled me with compassion for us all. I recognized Gandhi-gone-Gucci compatriots not only putting their money into what they believed, but also pitching tents so they could sleep on the ground in the wind and rain to emerge with previously unknown pride, and soreness.

I walked for my grandma and my aunt who did not survive their battles with cancer. A growing comfort with my choice to step into nothingness and live there for a while powered me from within. Those three days were a celebration of grace and values in motion, and at the time I didn't know that my life would soon overflow with those characteristics. In those three days, I walked every step of the sixty-mile course, and in the process, became a toddler.

The reason that mastering walking is such a major development is because it is the time when babies gain enough confidence and balance to set out on their own. This makes it a huge milestone towards independence, when personality really blossoms, and babyhood is left behind. While it's hard to look back and compare myself as an adult woman with the transition from babyhood, it really is a good metaphor.

While I had always been honest and direct, my personality blossomed further once I committed myself to complete authenticity. There was no more hiding or avoiding conflict for my own comfort. I became fully true to my own personality, spirit, and character.

My new independence of thought allowed me to revisit my dreams without the false limitations I had previously imposed on them. It was in this freedom that I explored and designed what I really wanted my life to be like, and from that basis, I would choose what I would pursue professionally.

For me, this was an entirely new paradigm. I started by creating a specific list of characteristics I absolutely wanted my life to have, including: the kind of mother I wanted to be; what I wanted my relationship with my husband to be like; that I would be a complete person, including a career; that I would work no more than part time; and my minimum income. It wasn't a long list and it didn't need to be. These intentions were written in stone, since these were the terms I would not compromise.

With the freedom to explore, and my list of intentions in hand, I rediscovered a profession I had been very interested in at a former time. I had told myself previously that I was too young to become an executive coach. In the meantime, I had let go of those kinds of self-limiting thoughts, and had indeed grown older and more experienced. I went through the best coaching training available becoming a certified professional coach in record time and because of the alignment in my life this was as natural as water flowing downhill. I have created my business to fit me, and the way I want to spend my time during this chapter of my life.

As I support leaders through coaching in becoming more fulfilled, effective, and skilled in their power, they tell me how my work creates a ripple effect on their families, the outlook of their entire organization and out into their communities. In what feels like a thumbs-up from the universe, opportunities grow around me like wildflowers in Spring.

My value of contribution is deeply fulfilled through my work supporting leaders in business and government and their organizations. These people already 'get it' and are seeking their next level of awareness, impact and leadership. The very best moments are when the realization comes that they don't have to wait to start living their dreams. Together, we create the plans for them to move into their bold legacy. With this, my contribution supports theirs and that synergy has a snowball effect.

My passion for business and the environment lives out in the work I do with socially responsible businesses, and in time, I dream of creating an institute for leaders in sustainability, offering seminars, retreats, and policy programs – and I will make this dream a reality in the next chapter of my life when I want to devote more time to my career. In this chapter I am enjoying fulfilling my covenant with my daughter and myself.

Speaking of which, I recognize the old tendencies toward overwork always lurking in the love I have for my business. To keep that in check, I have created some serious boundaries to make certain that I do not compromise on my integrity. For example, I work three, and only three, days a week. To ensure this, we're enrolled three days per week at an awesome daycare center. If I want to work more it can't just happen by accident, which slows my thinking enough to see the flashing yellow lights of my internal warning system. I've seen them plenty of times and they keep me from going over the line.

As a result, I now live my own bold legacy. I contribute to the lives of the people I touch professionally. I own a thriving business, and I am a fully engaged and present mom, partner and daughter. It may not make me Nelson Mandela...I'm also far from being done.

So let's turn our focus to you and your legacy. On a scale of 1 to 10, how much are you living the legacy of your choosing? Are you acting on your dreams? There are innumerable ways to live a bold legacy. You can seek political office and make an impact on public policy. You can create events like the three-day walk I participated in. Open that business you've been dreaming of. Start mentoring disadvantaged kids. Any vivid dream of yours can become a legacy when married to the action of screwing up the courage to put one foot in front of the other.

For those embarking on living a bold legacy and those of us already on the path there are a few obstacles that keep showing up. Here's my pocket survival guide:

Self-Limiting Thoughts

If you find the limiting voices in your head telling you that you can't do it, or can't do it now, you can combat them by using a not-so-secret weapon. Use the magic word, 'how.' Transform 'I can't do that' into 'How can I do that?' or 'I'd have to sacrifice my standard of living' into 'How can I create what I want now without sacrificing my lifestyle?' Another good way to combat self-limiting thoughts is to prove them wrong. Just look around you. People are doing amazing things all the time. Go out and collect evidence to support your dream.

Either-Or Thinking

This shows up as the belief that if I pursue one course of action, then I am slamming the door on other passions and areas of experience. Either-Or Thinking can be navigated by applying some creativity toward creating synergy among your areas of interest. Let all the pieces of your life and all your dreams coalesce in your vision, and in time they will start to fit together. For example, I love coaching, and at the same time, I want to be working to create greater environmental sustainability in business. In addition to the other work my company does, I have a specialty coaching practice and offer trainings for this field. This illustrates the kind of synergy I'm talking about. It's a home run.

Fear of Risk

In order to boldly pursue an opportunity, we travel a road laden with risk. Still, instead of asking yourself what you're risking by pursuing your bold legacy, ask yourself what's being risked by not pursuing it. One way to reconnect with your courage in the face of fear is to clarify the distinction between safety and comfort. It's one thing to stand in front of an oncoming tank in the pursuit of your passions; it's another thing altogether to miss some "must see TV". We can shoehorn ourselves out of our comfort zones with the support of friends, mentors, and coaches, as well as with a strong connection to the vision we are heading towards. So what about safety? That's a matter of personal choice as to how far we will put ourselves in the line of danger in living out our passions. The good news is that, in this case, we have a choice, which means that genuine safety lies within.

Procrastination

"I get your point Michelle, and I'm going to get to it right after…the kids grow up, I save more money, I figure out what I really want to do, (fill in the blank)." These are perfectly reasonable, even respectable, excuses. However they are still excuses. I'm not suggesting that you immediately put down this book, drive to the airport and leave for Tibet. Your plan might take two to three years to complete before you are living your legacy. However, what I am encouraging you to do is to begin to create your plan and start to put it into action. To live your BOLD legacy, let your daring spirit loose, paint your vision with your biggest dreams, then get into motion.

There are two parts to the calculation of legacy; it is made up of contribution and a life well led. A bold legacy is about delivering on both. When I started I grasped half of the equation and that miscalculation took its toll. From there I put the pieces back together to create a thriving, complete life that has become my bold legacy.

It took a lot of pain for me to get the message, and I'm sharing what I've learned because I don't believe anyone has to suffer to get the message. My back is broad and strong; this is an invitation to play leapfrog. The next move is up to you.

I'm here calling to you like John Cusack in that great cinematic moment in Say Anything; I'm holding up my boom box outside your window, calling to you, saying, "Now is your time. Come out and walk with me. We will find our footing, and our spirits will go soaring."

Highlights for living a bold legacy

- You are going to leave a legacy no matter what. Make it the one you want.
- A bold legacy is made up of two parts: contribution and how you live your life.
- Values can overwhelm each other. Choose how you want to align yours.
- Design how you want to live your life and make your work fit your life, not the other way around.
- Be intentional with characteristics for your life you won't compromise.
- Be yourself and be true to yourself.
- Start now!